WILLIAM BLAKE

The wood engraving reproduced above
is taken, with others in this book,
from a selection held at the
Victoria and Albert Museum, London.

WILLIAM BLAKE

SELECTED POEMS

WITH AN INTRODUCTION
BY DENIS SAURAT

WESTHOUSE
LONDON
1947

First published in May 1947 by

JOHN WESTHOUSE (PUBLISHERS LTD)
49 CHANCERY LANE
LONDON W C 2

Printed by H O LOESCHER LTD
70 Brewer Street London W 1

CONTENTS

Introduction

BLAKE is a very great poet—but— in fact, he is the greatest of English poets after, say, Chaucer, Spenser, Shakespeare and Milton. What a list! As a Frenchman, who feels proud to have been a guest in their country, I am tempted to say that there never was such a list in the world, all the more since it goes on— Yet, I reflect: Homer, Pindar, Æschylus, Sophocles, Euripides—and it comes to me: what a wonder to be a cultured man some time before A.D. 200, just under the Antonines, and add Virgil and Lucretius to those Greeks— and with a little luck, the Bible of the Jews in the Greek, and, with a little more luck still, perhaps, in that queerer Greek—and easier— some of those new Gospels, and some of that Paul's epistles, or that John's— To feel that an unbroken tradition of a thousand years links you to Homer; that there were still people in Greece that spoke more or less as Homer had spoken;—Jews running about that spoke as Moses;—and Christians who had known those that had known Paul—that Paul who had written to some Romans.

We must be humble, and even to-day say: those ancients were greater than we. And what other ancients may there not have been before them?

There is some similarity between our XIXth century and the century of the Antonines. Both were periods of great prosperity preceding a disintegration. Blake stands in bewilderment at the beginning of that period of ours: The first really great man to be in the position in which we are now, of not knowing what to think or what to feel or what to do. The Romans came to that about A.D. 300 and we about 1900. We are still under Blake's star.

Still, we have done well: Chaucer, Spenser, Shakespeare, Milton, Blake.

What of Blake? Verlaine, who knew not of him, judged well:

> Quelque chose du cœur enfantin et subtil—
> Et vraiment, quand la mort viendra, que reste-t-il?

A child's heart, and a childish heart, and a subtle heart. And one that knew something of that other side of death, which is the other side of life.

A very great poet—but, so often, a very bad poet. A child—and a nuisance. Psychic? Horrible word—it should mean: who has a soul—and has not everyone a soul? Alas, yes, Blake was psychic, in the horrible sense of the word. He saw things. Monstrous things and beings, that were, in part, not there; and that were, in part, more real than reality:

> things more real than mortal man.

And he raved—and he ranted—and he told lies.

A very great poet—but one in whose works it is more difficult to separate the chaff from the grain than in any other.

To most people Blake's short poems are his greatest achievement. I hope that the perusal of this book will induce some to believe that Blake achieved his highest in some passages of the long epics and that his short poems are really only his exercises before he reaches his full strength. But in his short poems we see already his characteristics. His discontent with reality as observed on Earth is perhaps his most striking trait. With it goes a conveyed impression of absolute sincerity which is sometimes absolutely effective. Only sometimes. For we also find in Blake decaying remnants of the previous classical mentality, in classical platitudes, and also much of the romantic nonsense that was becoming fashionable:

> Hear the voice of the Bard!
> Who Present, Past & Future, sees:

on the one hand, and:

> A little black thing among the snow,
> Crying 'weep! weep!' in notes of woe!

Perhaps what Blake contributes of his own is a sort of childish sensationalism of which he will never get cured and which is the bad side of that childlike fantasy and strength that produces

> Tyger! Tyger! burning bright
> In the forests of the night—

There is in Blake's poetry that curiously mixed element which makes *Treasure Island* and *Alice in Wonderland* books that are welcome both to the child and to the adult—slightly under false pretences in both categories. And yet reaching down to strata in the human being that

9

are common to both children and grown-ups. Perhaps what we appreciate most in Blake's shorter poems is his vision into what could be called the other side of things. This will lead to his sarcastic works which another category of readers (Samuel Butler and Bernard Shaw, for instance) will consider to be Blake's masterpieces: *The Marriage of Heaven and Hell* and *The Everlasting Gospel*. In the shorter poems, that on prostitutes—*London,* and that on motherhood—*To Tirza,* are perhaps the best examples. But this is dangerous from the literary point of view. It leads to cheap moralizing:

> How the youthful Harlot's curse
> Blasts the new born Infant's tear—

Blake also attaches too much importance to suffering and wallows rather a little too much in pity: pity for others which is apt to change into pity for himself.

Yet again Blake is inspired here by his deep feeling that desire is natural and legitimate and that repression is evil. One of his loveliest poems:

> I laid me down upon a bank
> Where love lay sleeping—

contains the seed of all our XXth-century psycho-analysis and goes even further into a new cosmology: the *thistles and thorns of the waste* are really human spirits that have been *driven out and compelled to be chaste*. Here is a conception of the creation of the outside world which is akin to and truer poetically and spiritually than Victor Hugo's conception that all outside objects are human souls expiating past crimes by being imprisoned into things and plants and animals. A formidable but mechanical vision. Blake's imaginings of the compulsion to be chaste producing thistles and thorns is much more in keeping with our own feeling that all repression is evil and that sins of omission are much more deadly than sins of commission.

But all this moralizing is at the most only material for literature. Literature needs good material, no doubt, but it needs above all the mastery of the language, the form that we call art. The sound and the rhythm, the strength and the simplicity and the truth, both in the detail of the words and in the composition of the poem. And Blake reaches great art by his mastery of language, form and composition:

> There is a smile of Love,
> And there is a smile of Deceit—

Two astonishing masterpieces, *The Mental Traveller* and *The Crystal Cabinet*, stand as peaks in literature. They are situated in a spiritual zone to which Mallarmé, eighty years later, hardly ever attained. All that tremendous cogitation which the French symbolists so admirably performed lay already in a semi-unconscious state in Blake's mind. It was perhaps all the better for being half unconscious, since the poems that Blake wrote in that mood are greater poems and more symbolistic in the Mallarméan sense than any of Mallarmé's. It is an astonishing event in the domain of the spirit that the achievements of symbolism should have been supremely successful in an English poet between 1790 and 1810 whereas the theory of symbolism, under which we still live, was worked out supremely well by a French poet who was completely ignorant of Blake, between 1870 and 1890. It looks nearly as though Providence had made a mistake and had intended Mallarmé to live a hundred years before Blake, say at the time of Herbert and Vaughan in England. This impression is reinforced by the fact that Mallarmé taught English for a living.

Fallen on evil days like Baudelaire's albatross on the deck of the ship:

> Ses ailes de géant l'empechent de marcher—

But Providence makes no mistakes. It inserted Blake into the English tradition because the English language alone could carry the full weight of symbols, since the French language is already too abstract. Mallarmé, mind you, tries to turn this into an advantage and says that the French language is the most poetical of all *because* it is the most abstract—but poor Mallarmé did not know English very well, in spite of his profession. Read:

> Je t'apporte l'enfant d'une nuit d'Idumée

and then read Blake's *Mental Traveller*. No doubt can be left. The English poem is a typhoon in the tropics, whereas the French poem is only a tempest in the North Atlantic.

Thus Providence sent Mallarmé a hundred years later than Blake so that Mallarmé could explain. And it is a part of the mad logicality of symbolism that Mallarmé was condemned to explain Blake whose writings he did not know. God thus proved himself to be a symbolist poet, just as in Sir James Jeans' theories God proves himself an exponent of the higher mathematics. In *The Mental Traveller* and *The Crystal Cabinet* perhaps we have Blake at his highest:

> He plants himself in all her nerves
> Just as a husbandman his mould;
> And she becomes his dwelling place
> And garden fruitful seventy fold.

But perhaps the highest of Blake is too high for human poetry and we cannot quite follow him. But that element will remain, later in the great poems when Blake will be at his most natural as well as at his highest:

> What is the price of Experience? Do men buy it for a song?

The *Auguries of Innocence—The Everlasting Gospel—* the *Marriage of Heaven and Hell*, and, from one angle, the *Visions of the Daughters of Albion* as a plea for free love, represent the XVIIIth-century element in Blake, sarcastic and critical. Just as in his symbolist poems Blake cuts the ground from under Mallarmé, in these moral essays and poems he cuts the ground from under Nietzsche. He is in fact as superior to Nietzsche as he is superior to Mallarmé. *The Marriage of Heaven and Hell* makes *Jenseits von Gute und Bose and Also Sprach Zarathustra* look from one side cheap and flat and from the other side bombastic, swollen and void. Yet let no one say that Nietzsche is not a great writer and a great poet; even as Mallarmé is also a great thinker and a great poet, but they are both adolescents when compared with Blake's maturity. Nietzsche may talk about putting morality upside down but he fails to do so: his feeble eulogy of force, his vain imaginings of the superman go down before any one of twenty or thirty of Blake's aphorisms:

> The soul of sweet delight can never be defiled—
> The fox provides for himself, but God provides for the lion.
> Joys impregnate. Sorrows bring forth.

Poor Nietzsche. Just as Mallarmé in a feeble attempt to convince himself had said that French was a more poetic language than English, Nietzsche, in an even feebler fit of ignorance, said that the English could not think. Whereas the whole of Nietzsche's thinking in his twenty-five volumes is put in the shade by a single page of Blake in *The Marriage of Heaven and Hell*. Nietzsche simply did not know that there was a spiritual side to things, whereas Blake lives and thinks in the spiritual side, even in his sarcasms.

And Blake's sarcasms are much more sarcastic than Nietzsche's.

And Blake has a sense of humour of which Nietzsche has only a caricature. For Blake was having a dart at himself in that *Memorable Fancy* when:

> The prophets Isaiah and Ezekiel dined with me, and I asked them how they dared so roundly to assert that God spoke to them; and whether they did not think at the time that they would be misunderstood, and so be the cause of imposition.
>
> Isaiah answered: ' I saw no God, nor heard any, in a finite organical perception; but my senses discovered the infinite in everything, and as I was then perswaded, & remain confirm'd, that the voice of honest indignation is the voice of God, I cared not for consequences, but wrote.'

In short, Blake is perfectly aware that, in a way, he is telling us lies, but he *cares not for consequences* and writes. Nietzsche was quite incapable of this self-criticism. And yet out of this sarcastic mood and of the honest indignation comes marvellous poetry in the *Visions of the Daughters of Albion* in which Blake transits into the epic mood:

> Does the whale worship at thy footsteps as the hungry dog?
> Or does he scent the mountain prey because his nostrils wide
> Draw in the ocean? Does his eye discern the flying cloud
> As the raven's eye? . . .
> The moment of desire! the moment of desire! The virgin
> That pines for man shall awaken her womb to enormous joys—
> Where the horrible darkness is impressed with reflections of
>   desire? . . .
> Thus every morning wails Oothoon; but Theotormon sits
> Upon the margin'd ocean conversing with shadows dire.

Let us now go:

Upon the margin'd ocean conversing with shadows dire—

Homer has no more powerful line, not even when Apollo is on that margin and shoots his plague darts into his victims' camp. Blake comes to his full power in the three great epics. All his supreme lyrics, all his powerful thinking on ethics and psychology are only preparations for his epic poetry. But unfortunately, in punishment of some ancient crime, the god Apollo from his position upon the margin'd ocean has directed his darts into Blake's country and far and away the larger part of Blake's country is in ruins. A few perfect monuments still stand here and there in the midst of desperate wastes. Let every reader who can search the deserts. Perhaps the brave reader will discover beauties other than those I have found. But here are those I have found, here are the fragments that seem to me great. They are few if we think of the three hundred and sixty-seven pages of the *Nonesuch Press* edition from which they come. But that is a wrong way to count. If you compare the number of magnificent lines which they contain with the number of lines which can be put in the same class in Milton, in Shakespeare, in Dante, and even in Virgil and Homer, you will find that Blake is indeed no mean peer in that company. The mischievous English workman of the first years of the XIXth century is no unworthy follower of the greatest.

Better perhaps than any other he has a sense of the eternal behind human feeling and moral values and also behind nature:

—and the awful Sun
Stands still upon the Mountain looking on the little Bird
With eyes of soft humility & wonder, love & awe—
—the Rose still sleeps,
None dare to wake her—

Also for the plain moral statement of devastating sincerity none sur-
pass Blake:

> It is an easy thing to triumph in the summer's sun—
> It is an easy thing to talk of patience to the afflicted,—

those are two elements of great poetry that will fuse into the spiritual
supreme in the last piece, on Christ. Add to it unexpected revelations
of spiritual realities not understood but incontrovertible:

> There is a Moment in each Day that Satan cannot find,
> Nor can his Watch Fiends find it;

(just as in the shorter poems there was that smile:)

> But, when it once is Smil'd,
> There's an end to all Misery.

But before we let ourselves go in praise, let us have a look at the
ruins round this St. Paul's Cathedral. They are ruins of three kinds,
all dreary and covering many miles:

> the mythology is all bad,
> the theories are all bad,
> the moral system is all bad.

That the mythology all arises from true visions during those years he
was at Felpham 'upon the margin'd ocean conversing with shadows
dire' makes no difference. A man can be a visionary and a bad poet. In
fact a visionary is practically always a bad poet: for instance, Swedenborg. There is only one point in literature where visions are success-
fully expressed: that is in the *New Testament*. Blake's visions therefore
are probably true in the sense that he saw them, but he was incapable
either of understanding or of describing them. To prove this I would
have to quote all that I have left out of this book. A few lines must
suffice as samples of bad poetry.

Tho' divided by the Cross & Nails & Thorns & Spear
In cruelties of Rahab & Tirzah, permanent endure
A terrible indefinite Hermaphroditic form,
A Wine-press of Love & Wrath, double, Hermaphroditic,
Twelvefold in Allegoric pomp, in selfish holiness:
The Pharisaion, the Grammateis, the Presbuterion,
The Archiereus, the Iereus, the Saddusaion: double
Each withoutside of the other, covering eastern heaven.

As for Blake's theories they are worse than his mythology. And when he describes how the ancient patriarchs came out of England before they took up their positions in Israel, what can we say to him?

Hyle dwelt in Winchester, comprehending Hants, Dorset, Devon, Cornwall,
Their Villages, Cities, Sea Ports, their Corn fields & Gardens spacious,
Palaces, Rivers & Mountains; and between Hand & Hyle arose
Gwendolen & Cambel who is Bodicea: they go abroad and return
Like lovely beams of light from the mingled affections of the Brothers.
The Inhabitants of the whole Earth rejoice in their beautiful light.
Coban dwelt in Bath: Somerset, Wiltshire, Gloucestershire
Obey'd his awful voice: Ignoge is his lovely Emanation;
She adjoin'd with Gwantoke's children; soon lovely Cordella arose;
Gwantoke forgave & joy'd over South Wales & all its Mountains.

Peachey had North Wales, Shropshire, Cheshire & the Isle of
   Man;
His Emanation is Mehetabel, terrible and lovely upon the
   Mountains.

But his worst and most insidious badness is in his moral system
which he camouflages into what we would call a psychological one.
Those four mighty ones that are in every man, that Urizen, that Thar-
mes, that Los, and that Luvah, beware of them. And more particularly
when they begin to have emanations and spectres and divide themselves into male and female with something left over. Do beware of
them. They invariably fall into rages and talk the most abominable
fustian:

Then Orc cried: Curse thy cold hypocrisy! already round
   thy tree
In scales that shine with gold and rubies, thou beginnest to
   weaken
My divided spirit. Like a worm I rise in peace, unbound
From wrath. Now when I rage, my fetters bind me more.
O torment! O torment! A Worm compell'd! Am I a worm?
Is it in strong deceit that man is born? In strong deceit
Thou dost restrain my fury that the worm may fold the tree.
Avaunt, cold hypocrite! I am chain'd, or thou couldst not use
   me thus.
The Man shall rage, bound with this chain, the worm in
   silence creep.
Thou wilt not cease from rage. Grey demon, silence all thy
   storms.

And I dare not for very shame do more than hint at what Washington spoke, or the queen of the French, for Blake is at his steady worst when he goes into history; so here is narrative:

> Solemn heave the Atlantic waves between the gloomy nations,
> Swelling, belching from its deeps red clouds & raging fires.
> Albion is sick! America faints! enrag'd the Zenith grew.
> As human blood shooting its veins all round the orbed heaven,
> Red rose the clouds from the Atlantic in vast wheels of blood,
> And in the red clouds rose a Wonder o'er the Atlantic sea,
> Intense! naked! a Human fire, fierce glowing, as the wedge
> Of iron heated in the furnace: his terrible limbs were fire
> With myriads of cloudy terrors, banners dark & towers
> Surrounded: heat but not light went thro' the murky atmo-
> sphere.

And Blake's crimes are made the greater because here and there he inserts unwittingly a lovely or a powerful line. We cannot deny that there are roses in his desert, but excerpts of one line are not long enough for anthologies. They are the rewards that await the weary traveller courageous enough to go through the desert. Here we give only the oasis with at least ten or twelve trees in each and a spring of water. One unnatural rose at a time is not enough.

No doubt tribes and countries do exist, no doubt quarrels do occur, and schizophrenia—but not as he says. He has a bad subject and he presents it badly.

But let us turn from these painful though salutary considerations to the great things. Blake reaches also the highest descriptive poetry:

> Albion cold lays on his Rock: storms and snows beat round
> him,
> Beneath the Furnaces & the starry Wheels & the Immortal
> Tomb:

> Howling winds cover him: roaring seas dash furious against
> him:
> In the deep darkness broad lightnings glare, long thunders
> roll.
> The weeds of Death inwrap his hands & feet, blown incessant
> And wash'd incessant by the for-ever restless sea-waves foaming
> abroad
> Upon the white Rock.

And at his highest he reaches at the same time power, simplicity, and
the purest spiritual value. The miracle of Joseph and Mary is worthy
of the best of the miracles of the Middle Ages before literature began:

> She looked & saw Joseph the Carpenter in Nazareth & Mary
> His espoused Wife. And Mary said, 'If thou put me away from
> thee
> Dost thou not murder me?' Joseph spoke in anger & fury,
> 'Should I
> Marry a Harlot & an Adulteress?' Mary answer'd, 'Art thou
> more pure
> Than thy Maker who forgiveth Sins & calls again Her that is
> Lost?'

Above all futile complications of history and intellect, here we reach
essential reality. Higher still and highest is that last conversation between Jesus and Albion when the secret of the world is revealed to
Blake:

Why had Jesus to die and therefore why has man to suffer? The two
are connected. Men suffer a little in order to help Jesus to bear the
passion and the death. Because it is suffering that creates love. God

20

created the world by tearing it out of himself and dying in suffering. Man helps God to create the world when man suffers:

> Jesus said: 'Wouldest thou love one who never died
> For thee, or ever die for one who had not died for thee?
> And if God dieth not for Man & giveth not himself
> Eternally for Man, Man could not exist; for Man is Love
> As God is Love: every kindness to another is a little Death
> In the Divine Image, nor can Man exist but by Brotherhood.'

Here realistic common sense is united to the deepest spiritual insight. The language is simple and powerful. There is no added mythology, no system. A deep and obscure moral intuition is put into powerful and direct language. The nearer Blake comes to being a Christian, the greater poet he is: that is to say, when he expounds deeper meanings in the ordinary forms of Christianity. When he gives up his artificialities and his errors. Child of the XVIIIth century though he is, he needs the maternal bosom of the Christian faith. He is the naughty child of a wicked father by a good mother. He runs away and gets into frightful messes with his bad urchin friends Urizen and Los, and then he comes back to his mother to be washed and put to bed and have lovely dreams.

We are in the same disorder as Blake was and as his contemporaries were, both outside and inside. Our wars of to-day are in a different form from the wars of the great revolution and of the Napoleonic era, and this outside state of chaos and violence is only as in Blake's time the outside representation of the bewilderment within the men and the women of to-day.

We also have lost all our beliefs and are looking in vain for new ones.

How can Blake then help us?

When he succeeds, he can help us to see suffering as a hard way to a greater reality and to a benevolent reality. He can convince us if we meditate on his case that we need deeply a change in ethics, both in our theory and in our practice. He may be able to teach us far better than Nietzsche how to emerge into simplicity out of bewilderment, on essential questions. For instance, on our sexual problem, which is perhaps destroying us.

Also, and not least, he can teach us if we are careful pupils, how to give artistic form to chaos. Chaos under our will can be productive of form and beauty. Blake can point the way to that new art that we are looking for. But he is a dangerous teacher. He has not separated the good from the bad in art, and are we not at that stage? Now? What of Picasso?

'The eye sees more than the heart knows', says Blake; it is the duty of each one of us to discriminate. And we are in the same danger as Blake. May his many downfalls be lessons to us. Seeing the rubbish in his poems, let us try and avoid building structures that are condemned to become rubbish. Nothing can be so bad for us as indiscriminate admiration for Blake, as our great dangers are very similar to the dangers that so often overcame him. He is our *terrible warning*. But, on the other hand, nothing can be so directly helpful to us as his really good things, because they are in the direction of the way out of our troubles.

When Milton is not acceptable to us Blake can sometimes help.

By recognizing the passages where he wins through into clear simplicity we can help ourselves both morally and artistically. His fear-

22

lessness is perhaps the most useful example he can give us, but he has it only in rare moments. Often he is bewildered and frightened; let us not accept him then but pity him. He wins through; let us try and win through.

This book is an attempt to choose those passages in which he wins through and to isolate them from the deleterious rubbish. The test is literary; there is none other. This is the greatest function of literature, that it can sort the good from the bad: the pure parts of the New Testament are by far the highest literature of the world. This is therefore a presentation of Blake as one man who is trying to be internationally minded sees him, purely from a literary point of view. Here is Meredith's test applied even to the so-called *spirit*:

Is it accepted of song?

Does it run with disciplined feet?

Here are the disciplined feet of Blake coming over the hills of a hundred and fifty years

Nurse's Song

WHEN the voices of children are heard on the green
And whisp'rings are in the dale,
The days of my youth rise fresh in my mind,
My face turns green and pale

Then come home, my children, the sun is gone down,
And the dews of night arise;
Your spring & your day are wasted in play,
And your winter and night in disguise

The Sick Rose

O ROSE, thou art sick!
The invisible worm
That flies in the night,
In the howling storm,

Has found out thy bed
Of crimson joy,
And his dark secret love
Does thy life destroy

The Tyger

TYGER! Tyger! burning bright
In the forests of the night,
What immortal hand or eye
Could frame thy fearful symmetry?

In what distant deeps or skies
Burnt the fire of thine eyes?
On what wings dare he aspire?
What the hand dare sieze the fire?

And what shoulder, & what art,
Could twist the sinews of thy heart?
And when thy heart began to beat,
What dread hand? & what dread feet?

What the hammer? what the chain?
In what furnace was thy brain?
What the anvil? what dread grasp
Dare its deadly terrors clasp?

When the stars threw down their spears,
And water'd heaven with their tears,
Did he smile his work to see?
Did he who made the Lamb make thee?

Tyger! Tyger! burning bright
In the forests of the night,
What immortal hand or eye
Dare frame thy fearful symmetry?

London

I WANDER thro' each charter'd street,
Near where the charter'd Thames does flow,
And mark in every face I meet
Marks of weakness, marks of woe

In every cry of every Man,
In every Infant's cry of fear,
In every voice, in every ban,
The mind-forg'd manacles I hear

How the Chimney-sweeper's cry
Every black'ning Church appalls;
And the hapless Soldier's sigh
Runs in blood down Palace walls

But most thro' midnight streets I hear
How the youthful Harlot's curse
Blasts the new born Infant's tear,
And blights with plagues the Marriage hearse

Infant Sorrow

MY mother groan'd! my father wept
Into the dangerous world I leapt:
Helpless, naked, piping loud:
Like a fiend hid in a cloud

Struggling in my father's hands,
Striving against my swadling bands,
Bound and weary I thought best
To sulk upon my mother's breast

A Poison Tree

I WAS angry with my friend:
I told my wrath, my wrath did end.
I was angry with my foe:
I told it not, my wrath did grow.

And I water'd it in fears,
Night & morning with my tears;
And I sunned it with smiles,
And with soft deceitful wiles

And it grew both day and night,
Till it bore an apple bright;
And my foe beheld it shine,
And he knew that it was mine

And into my garden stole
When the night had veil'd the pole:
In the morning glad I see
My foe outstretch'd beneath the tree

To Tirzah

WHATE'ER is Born of Mortal Birth
Must be consumed with the Earth
To rise from Generation free:
Then what have I to do with thee?

29

The Sexes sprung from Shame & Pride,
Blow'd in the morn; in evening died;
But Mercy chang'd Death into Sleep;
The Sexes rose to work & weep

Thou, Mother of my Mortal part,
With cruelty didst mould my Heart,
And with false self-decieving tears
Didst bind my Nostrils, Eyes, & Ears:

Didst close my Tongue in senseless clay,
And me to Mortal Life betray.
The Death of Jesus set me free:
Then what have I to do with thee?

Poems From MSS

Written about 1793

¶

NEVER seek to tell thy love
Love that never told can be;
For the gentle wind does move
Silently, invisibly

I told my love, I told my love,
I told her all my heart,
Trembling, cold, in ghastly fears—
Ah, she doth depart

30

Soon as she was gone from me
A traveller came by
Silently, invisibly—
O, was no deny

¶

I LAID me down upon a bank
Where love lay sleeping.
I heard among the rushes dank
Weeping, Weeping

Then I went to the heath & the wild
To the thistles & thorns of the waste
And they told me how they were beguil'd,
Driven out, & compel'd to be chaste

¶

I ASKED a thief to steal me a peach:
He turned up his eyes.
I ask'd a lithe lady to lie her down:
Holy & meek she cries

As soon as I went an angel came:
He wink'd at the thief
And smil'd at the dame,
And without one word spoke
Had a peach from the tree,
And 'twixt earnest & joke
Enjoy'd the Lady

31

¶

ABSTINENCE SOWS sand all over
The ruddy limbs & flaming hair,
But Desire Gratified
Plants fruits of life & beauty there

¶

IN a wife I would desire
What in whores is always found—
The lineaments of Gratified desire

¶

IF you trap the moment before it's ripe,
The tears of repentance you'll certainly wipe;
But if once you let the ripe moment go
You can never wipe off the tears of woe

Eternity

HE who binds to himself a joy
Does the winged life destroy;
But he who kisses the joy as it flies
Lives in eternity's sun rise

The Question Answer'd

WHAT is it men in women do require?
The lineaments of Gratified Desire.
What is it women do in men require?
The lineaments of Gratified Desire

¶

EACH Man is in his Spectre's power
Untill the arrival of that hour,
When his Humanity awake
And cast his own Spectre into the Lake

Poems written about 1803

The Smile

THERE is a Smile of Love,
And there is a Smile of Deceit,
And there is a Smile of Smiles
In which these two Smiles meet

And there is a Frown of Hate,
And there is a Frown of Disdain,
And there is a Frown of Frowns
Which you strive to forget in vain,

For it sticks in the Heart's deep Core
And it sticks in the deep Back bone;
And no Smile that ever was smil'd,
But only one Smile alone,

That betwixt the Cradle & Grave
It only once Smil'd can be;
But, when it once is Smil'd,
There's an end to all Misery

The Mental Traveller

I TRAVEL'D thro' a Land of Men,
A Land of Men & Women too,
And heard & saw such dreadful things
As cold Earth wanderers never knew

For there the Babe is born in joy
That was begotten in dire woe;
Just as we Reap in joy the fruit
Which we in bitter tears did sow

And if the Babe is born a Boy
He's given to a Woman Old,
Who nails him down upon a rock,
Catches his shrieks in cups of gold

She binds iron thorns around his head,
She pierces both his hands & feet,
She cuts his heart out at his side
To make it feel both cold & heat

Her fingers number every Nerve,
Just as a Miser counts his gold;
She lives upon his shrieks & cries,
And she grows young as he grows old

Till he becomes a bleeding youth,
And she becomes a Virgin bright;
Then he rends up his Manacles
And binds her down for his delight

He plants himself in all her Nerves,
Just as a Husbandman his mould;
And she becomes his dwelling place
And Garden fruitful seventy fold

An aged Shadow, soon he fades,
Wand'ring round an Earthly Cot,
Full filled all with gems & gold
Which he by industry had got

And these are the gems of the Human Soul,
The rubies & pearls of a lovesick eye,
The countless gold of the akeing heart,
The martyr's groan & the lover's sigh

They are his meat, they are his drink;
He feeds the Beggar & the Poor
And the wayfaring Traveller:
For ever open is his door

His grief is their eternal joy;
They make the roofs & walls to ring;
Till from the fire on the hearth
A little Female Babe does spring

And she is all of solid fire
And gems & gold, that none his hand
Dares stretch to touch her Baby form,
Or wrap her in his swaddling-band

But She comes to the Man she loves,
If young or old, or rich or poor;
They soon drive out the aged Host,
A Beggar at another's door

He wanders weeping far away,
Untill some other take him in;
Oft blind & age-bent, sore distrest,
Untill he can a Maiden win

And to allay his freezing Age
The Poor Man takes her in his arms;
The Cottage fades before his sight,
The Garden & its lovely Charms

The Guests are scatter'd thro' the land,
For the Eye altering alters all;
The Senses roll themselves in fear,
And the flat Earth becomes a Ball;

The stars, sun, Moon, all shrink away,
A desart vast without a bound,
And nothing left to eat or drink,
And a dark desart all around

The honey of her Infant lips,
The bread & wine of her sweet smile,
The wild game of her roving Eye,
Does him to Infancy beguile;

For as he eats & drinks he grows
Younger & younger every day;
And on the desart wild they both
Wander in terror & dismay

Like the wild Stag she flees away,
Her fear plants many a thicket wild;
While he pursues her night & day,
By various arts of Love beguil'd,

By various arts of Love & Hate,
Till the wide desart planted o'er
With Labyrinths of wayward Love,
Where roam the Lion, Wolf & Boar,

Till he becomes a wayward Babe,
And she a weeping Woman Old.
Then many a Lover wanders here;
The Sun & Stars are nearer roll'd

The trees bring forth sweet Extacy
To all who in the desart roam;
Till many a City there is Built,
And many a pleasant Shepherd's home

But when they find the frowning Babe,
Terror strikes thro' the region wide:
They cry "The Babe! the Babe is Born!"
And flee away on Every side

For who dare touch the frowning form,
His arm is wither'd to its root;
Lions, Boars, Wolves, all howling flee,
And every Tree does shed its fruit

And none can touch that frowning form,
Except it be a Woman Old;
She nails him down upon the Rock,
And all is done as I have told

The Crystal Cabinet

THE Maiden caught me in the Wild,
Where I was dancing merrily;
She put me into her Cabinet
And Lock'd me up with a golden Key

This Cabinet is form'd of Gold
And Pearl & Crystal shining bright,
And within it opens into a World
And a little lovely Moony Night

Another England there I saw,
Another London with its Tower,
Another Thames & other Hills,
And another pleasant Surrey Bower,

Another Maiden like herself,
Translucent, lovely, shining clear,
Threefold each in the other clos'd—
O, what a pleasant trembling fear!

O, what a smile! a threefold Smile
Fill'd me, that like a flame I burn'd;
I bent to Kiss the lovely Maid,
And found a Threefold Kiss return'd

I strove to sieze the inmost Form
With ardor fierce & hands of flame,
But burst the Crystal Cabinet,
And like a Weeping Babe became—

A weeping Babe upon the wild,
And Weeping Woman pale reclin'd,
And in the outward air again
I fill'd with woes the passing Wind

Auguries of Innocence

TO see a World in a Grain of Sand
And a Heaven in a Wild Flower,
Hold Infinity in the palm of your hand
And Eternity in an hour

A Robin Red breast in a Cage
Puts all Heaven in a Rage.
A dove house fill'd with doves & Pigeons
Shudders Hell thro' all its regions.
A dog starv'd at his Master's Gate
Predicts the ruin of the State.
A Horse misus'd upon the Road
Calls to Heaven for Human blood.

Each outcry of the hunted Hare
A fibre from the Brain does tear.
A Skylark wounded in the wing,
A Cherubim does cease to sing.
The Game Cock clip'd & arm'd for fight
Does the Rising Sun affright.
Every Wolf's & Lion's howl
Raises from Hell a Human Soul.
The wild deer, wand'ring here & there,
Keeps the Human Soul from Care
The Lamb misus'd breeds Public strife
And yet forgives the Butcher's Knife.
The Bat that flits at close of Eve
Has left the Brain that won't Believe.
The Owl that calls upon the Night
Speaks the Unbeliever's fright.
He who shall hurt the little Wren
Shall never be belov'd by Men.
He who the Ox to wrath has mov'd
Shall never be by Woman lov'd.
The wanton Boy that kills the Fly
Shall feel the Spider's enmity.
He who torments the Chafer's sprite
Weaves a Bower in endless Night.
The Catterpiller on the Leaf
Repeats to thee thy Mother's grief.
Kill not the Moth nor Butterfly,
For the Last Judgment draweth nigh.
He who shall train the Horse to War

Shall never pass the Polar Bar.
The Beggar's Dog & Widow's Cat,
Feed them & thou wilt grow fat.
The Gnat that sings his Summer's song
Poison gets from Slander's tongue.
The poison of the Snake & Newt
Is the sweat of Envy's Foot.
The Poison of the Honey Bee
Is the Artist's Jealousy.
The Prince's Robes & Beggar's Rags
Are Toadstools on the Miser's Bags.
A truth that's told with bad intent
Beats all the Lies you can invent.
It is right it should be so;
Man was made for Joy & Woe;
And when this we rightly know
Thro' the World we safely go,
Joy & Woe are woven fine,
A Clothing for the Soul divine;
Under every grief & pine
Runs a joy with silken twine.
The Babe is more than swadling Bands;
Throughout all these Human Lands
Tools were made, & Born were hands,
Every Farmer Understands.
Every Tear from Every Eye
Becomes a Babe in Eternity;
This is caught by Females bright
And return'd to its own delight.

The Bleat, the Bark, Bellow & Roar
Are Waves that Beat on Heaven's Shore.
The Babe that weeps the Rod beneath
Writes Revenge in realms of death.
The Beggar's Rags, fluttering in Air,
Does to Rags the Heavens tear.
The Soldier, arm'd with Sword & Gun,
Palsied strikes the Summer's Sun.
The poor Man's Farthing is worth more
Than all the Gold on Afric's Shore.
One Mite wrung from the Labrer's hands
Shall buy & sell the Miser's Lands:
Or, if protected from on high,
Does that whole Nation sell & buy.
He who mocks the Infant's Faith
Shall be mock'd in Age & Death.
He who shall teach the Child to Doubt
The rotting Grave shall ne'er get out.
He who respects the Infant's faith
Triumphs over Hell & Death.
The Child's Toys & the Old Man's Reasons
Are the Fruits of the Two seasons.
The Questioner, who sits so sly,
Shall never know how to Reply.
He who replies to words of Doubt
Doth put the Light of Knowledge out.
The Strongest Poison ever known
Came from Caesar's Laurel Crown.
Nought can deform the Human Race

Like to the Armour's iron brace.
When Gold & Gems adorn the Plow
To peaceful Arts shall Envy Bow.
A Riddle or the Cricket's Cry
Is to Doubt a fit Reply.
The Emmet's Inch & Eagle's Mile
Make Lame Philosophy to smile.
He who Doubts from what he sees
Will ne'er Believe, do what you Please.
If the Sun & Moon should doubt,
They'd immediately Go out.
To be in a Passion you Good may do,
But no Good if a Passion is in you.
The Whore & Gambler, by the State
Licenc'd, build that Nation's Fate.
The Harlot's cry from Street to Street
Shall weave Old England's winding Sheet.
The Winner's Shout, the Loser's Curse,
Dance before dead England's Hearse.
Every Night & every Morn
Some to Misery are Born.
Every Morn & every Night
Some are Born to sweet delight.
Some are Born to sweet delight,
Some are Born to Endless Night.
We are led to Believe a Lie
When we see not Thro' the Eye
Which was Born in a Night to perish in a Night
When the Soul Slept in Beams of Light.

God Appears & God is Light
To those poor Souls who dwell in Night,
But does a Human Form Display
To those who Dwell in Realms of day

¶

WHY was Cupid a Boy
And why a boy was he?
He should have been a Girl
For ought that I can see

For he shoots with his bow,
And the Girl shoots with her Eye,
And they both are merry & glad
And laugh when we do cry

And to make Cupid a Boy
Was the Cupid Girl's mocking plan;
For a boy can't interpret the thing
Till he is become a man

And then he's so pierc'd with cares
And wounded with arrowy smarts,
That the whole business of his life
Is to pick out the heads of the darts

'Twas the Greeks' love of war
Turn'd Love into a Boy,
And Woman into a Statue of Stone—
And away flew every Joy

46

THE MARRIAGE OF HEAVEN AND HELL

Etched about 1793

The Argument

RINTRAH roars & shakes his fires in the burden'd air;
Hungry clouds swag on the deep.

Once meek, and in a perilous path,
The just man kept his course along
The vale of death.
Roses are planted where thorns grow,
And on the barren heath
Sing the honey bees

Then the perilous path was planted,
And a river and a spring
On every cliff and tomb,
And on the bleached bones
Red clay brought forth;

Till the villain left the paths of ease,
To walk in perilous paths, and drive
The just man into barren climes

Now the sneaking serpent walks
In mild humility,
And the just man rages in the wilds
Where lions roam

Rintrah roars & shakes his fires in the burden'd air;
Hungry clouds swag on the deep

AS a new heaven is begun, and it is now thirty-three years since its advent, the Eternal Hell revives. And lo! Swedenborg is the Angel sitting at the tomb: his writings are the linen clothes folded up. Now is the dominion of Edom, & the return of Adam into Paradise. See Isaiah xxxiv & xxxv Chap.

Without Contraries is no progression. Attraction and Repulsion, Reason and Energy, Love and Hate, are necessary to Human existence.

From these contraries spring what the religious call Good & Evil. Good is the passive that obeys Reason. Evil is the active springing from Energy.

Good is Heaven. Evil is Hell.

The Voice of the Devil

ALL Bibles or sacred codes have been the causes of the following Errors:

1. That Man has two real existing principles: Viz: a Body & a Soul.

2. That Energy, call'd Evil, is alone from the Body; & that Reason, call'd Good, is alone from the Soul.

3. That God will torment Man in Eternity for following his Energies.

But the following Contraries to these are True:

1. Man has no Body distinct from his Soul; for that call'd Body is a portion of Soul discern'd by the five Senses, the chief inlets of Soul in this age.

2. Energy is the only life, and is from the Body; and Reason is the bound or outward circumference of Energy.

3. Energy is Eternal Delight.

48

THOSE who restrain desire, do so because theirs is weak enough to be restrained; and the restrainer or reason usurps its place & governs the unwilling.

And being restrain'd, it by degrees becomes passive, till it is only the shadow of desire.

The history of this is written in Paradise Lost, & the Governor or Reason is call'd Messiah.

And the original Archangel, or possessor of the command of the heavenly host, is call'd the Devil or Satan, and his children are call'd Sin & Death.

But in the Book of Job, Milton's Messiah is call'd Satan.

For this history has been adopted by both parties.

It indeed appear'd to Reason as if Desire was cast out; but the Devil's account is, that the Messiah fell, & formed a heaven of what he stole from the Abyss.

This is shewn in the Gospel, where he prays to the Father to send the comforter, or Desire, that Reason may have Ideas to build on; the Jehovah of the Bible being no other than he who dwells in flaming fire.

Know that after Christ's death, he became Jehovah.

But in Milton, the Father is Destiny, the Son a Ratio of the five senses, & the Holy-ghost Vacuum!

Note: The reason Milton wrote in fetters when he wrote of Angels & God, and at liberty when of Devils & Hell, is because he was a true Poet and of the Devil's party without knowing it.

A Memorable Fancy

AS I was walking among the fires of hell, delighted with the enjoyments of Genius, which to Angels look like torment and insanity, I collected some of their Proverbs; thinking that as the sayings used in a nation mark its character, so the Proverbs of Hell show the nature of Infernal wisdom better than any description of buildings or garments.

When I came home: on the abyss of the five senses, where a flat sided steep frowns over the present world, I saw a mighty Devil folded in black clouds, hovering on the sides of the rock: with corroding fires he wrote the following sentence now perceived by the minds of men, & read by them on earth:

How do you know but ev'ry Bird that cuts the airy way,
Is an immense world of delight, clos'd by your senses five?

Proverbs of Hell

IN seed time learn, in harvest teach, in winter enjoy.
Drive your cart and your plow over the bones of the dead.
The road of excess leads to the palace of wisdom.
Prudence is a rich, ugly old maid courted by Incapacity.
He who desires but acts not, breeds pestilence.
The cut worm forgives the plow.
Dip him in the river who loves water.
A fool sees not the same tree that a wise man sees.
He whose face gives no light, shall never become a star.
Eternity is in love with the productions of time.
The busy bee has no time for sorrow.

The hours of folly are measur'd by the clock; but of wisdom, no clock can measure.

All wholesome food is caught without a net or a trap.

Bring out number, weight & measure in a year of dearth.

No bird soars too high, if he soars with his own wings.

A dead body revenges not injuries.

The most sublime act is to set another before you.

If the fool would persist in his folly he would become wise.

Folly is the cloke of knavery.

Shame is Pride's cloke.

Prisons are built with stones of Law, Brothels with bricks of Religion.

The pride of the peacock is the glory of God.

The lust of the goat is the bounty of God.

The wrath of the lion is the wisdom of God.

The nakedness of woman is the work of God.

Excess of sorrow laughs. Excess of joy weeps.

The roaring of lions, the howling of wolves, the raging of the stormy sea, and the destructive sword, are portions of eternity, too great for the eye of man.

The fox condemns the trap, not himself.

Joys impregnate. Sorrows bring forth.

Let man wear the fell of the lion, woman the fleece of the sheep.

The bird a nest, the spider a web, man friendship.

The selfish, smiling fool, & the sullen, frowning fool shall be both thought wise, that they may be a rod.

What is now proved was once only imagin'd.

The rat, the mouse, the fox, the rabbet watch the roots; the lion, the tyger, the horse, the elephant watch the fruits.

The cistern contains: the fountain overflows.

One thought fills immensity.

Always be ready to speak your mind, and a base man will avoid you.

Every thing possible to be believ'd is an image of truth.

The eagle never lost so much time as when he submitted to learn of the crow.

The fox provides for himself, but God provides for the lion.

Think in the morning. Act in the noon. Eat in the evening. Sleep in the night.

He who has suffer'd you to impose on him, knows you.

As the plow follows words, so God rewards prayers.

The tygers of wrath are wiser than the horses of instruction.

Expect poison from the standing water.

You never know what is enough unless you know what is more than enough.

Listen to the fool's reproach! it is a kingly title!

The eyes of fire, the nostrils of air, the mouth of water, the beard of earth.

The weak in courage is strong in cunning.

The apple tree never asks the beech how he shall grow; nor the lion, the horse, how he shall take his prey.

The thankful reciever bears a plentiful harvest.

If others had not been foolish, we should be so.

The soul of sweet delight can never be defil'd.

When thou seest an Eagle, thou seest a portion of Genius; lift up thy head!

As the caterpiller chooses the fairest leaves to lay her eggs on, so the priest lays his curse on the fairest joys.

To create a little flower is the labour of ages.

52

Damn braces. Bless relaxes.

The best wine is the oldest, the best water the newest.

Prayers plow not! Praises reap not!

Joys laugh not! Sorrows weep not!

The head Sublime, the heart Pathos, the genitals Beauty, the hands & feet Proportion.

As the air to a bird or the sea to a fish, so is contempt to the contemptible.

The crow wish'd every thing was black, the owl that every thing was white.

Exuberance is Beauty.

If the lion was advised by the fox, he would be cunning.

Improvement makes strait roads; but the crooked roads without Improvement are roads of Genius.

Sooner murder an infant in its cradle than nurse unacted desires.

Where man is not, nature is barren.

Truth can never be told so as to be understood, and not be believ'd.

Enough! or Too much.

¶

THE ancient Poets animated all sensible objects with Gods or Geniuses, calling them by the names and adorning them with the properties of woods, rivers, mountains, lakes, cities, nations, and whatever their enlarged & numerous senses could percieve.

And particularly they studied the genius of each city & country, placing it under its mental deity;

Till a system was formed, which some took advantage of, & enslav'd the vulgar by attempting to realize or abstract the mental deities from their objects: thus began Priesthood;

54

Choosing forms of worship from poetic tales.

And at length they pronounc'd that the Gods had order'd such things.

Thus men forgot that All deities reside in the human breast.

A Memorable Fancy

THE Prophets Isaiah and Ezekiel dined with me, and I asked them how they dared so roundly to assert that God spoke to them; and whether they did not think at the time that they would be misunderstood, & so be the cause of imposition.

Isaiah answer'd: "I saw no God, nor heard any, in a finite organical "perception; but my senses discover'd the infinite in everything, and "as I was then perswaded, & remain confirm'd, that the voice of "honest indignation is the voice of God, I cared not for consequences, "but wrote."

Then I asked: "does a firm perswasion that a thing is so, make "it so?"

He replied: "All poets believe that it does, & in ages of imagina-"tion this firm perswasion removed mountains; but many are not "capable of a firm perswasion of any thing."

Then Ezekiel said: "The philosophy of the east taught the first "principles of human perception: some nations held one principle "for the origin, and some another: we of Israel taught that the Poetic "Genius (as you now call it) was the first principle and all the others "merely derivative, which was the cause of our despising the Priests "& Philosophers of other countries, and prophecying that all Gods "would at last be proved to originate in ours & to be the tributaries "of the Poetic Genius; it was this that our great poet, King David,

"desired so fervently & invokes so pathetic'ly, saying by this he
"conquers enemies & governs kingdoms; and we so loved our God,
"that we cursed in his name all the deities of surrounding nations,
"and asserted that they had rebelled: from these opinions the vulgar
"came to think that all nations would at last be subject to the jews."

"This," said he, "like all firm perswasions, is come to pass; for
"all nations believe the jews' code and worship the jews' god, and
"what greater subjection can be?"

I heard this with some wonder, & must confess my own conviction.
After dinner I ask'd Isaiah to favour the world with his lost works;
he said none of equal value was lost. Ezekiel said the same of his.

I also asked Isaiah what made him go naked and barefoot three
years? he answer'd: "the same that made our friend Diogenes, the
"Grecian."

I then asked Ezekiel why he eat dung, & lay so long on his right &
left side? he answer'd, "the desire of raising other men into a per-
"ception of the infinite: this the North American tribes practise, & is
"he honest who resists his genius or conscience only for the sake of
"present ease or gratification?"

¶

THE ancient tradition that the world will be consumed in fire at the
end of six thousand years is true, as I have heard from Hell.

For the cherub with his flaming sword is hereby commanded to
leave his guard at tree of life; and when he does, the whole creation
will be consumed and appear infinite and holy, whereas it now appears
finite & corrupt.

This will come to pass by an improvement of sensual enjoyment.

But first the notion that man has a body distinct from his soul is to

56

be expunged; this I shall do by printing in the infernal method, by corrosives, which in Hell are salutary and medicinal, melting apparent surfaces away, and displaying the infinite which was hid.

If the doors of perception were cleansed every thing would appear to man as it is, infinite.

For man has closed himself up, till he sees all things thro' narrow chinks of his cavern.

A Memorable Fancy

I WAS in a Printing house in Hell, & saw the method in which knowledge is transmitted from generation to generation.

In the first chamber was a Dragon-Man, clearing away the rubbish from a cave's mouth; within, a number of Dragons were hollowing the cave.

In the second chamber was a Viper folding round the rock & the cave, and others adorning it with gold, silver and precious stones.

In the third chamber was an Eagle with wings and feathers of air: he caused the inside of the cave to be infinite; around were numbers of Eagle-like men who built palaces in the immense cliffs.

In the fourth chamber were Lions of flaming fire, raging around & melting the metals into living fluids.

In the fifth chamber were Unnam'd forms, which cast the metals into the expanse.

There they were reciev'd by Men who occupied the sixth chamber, and took the forms of books & were arranged in libraries.

¶

THE Giants who formed this world into its sensual existence, and now seem to live in it in chains, are in truth the causes of its life & the sources of all activity; but the chains are the cunning of weak and tame minds which have power to resist energy; according to the proverb, the weak in courage is strong in cunning.

Thus one portion of being is the Prolific, the other the Devouring: to the Devourer it seems as if the producer was in his chains; but it is not so, he only takes portions of existence and fancies that the whole.

But the Prolific would cease to be Prolific unless the Devourer, as a sea, received the excess of his delights.

Some will say: "Is not God alone the Prolific?" I answer: "God "only Acts & Is, in existing beings or Men."

These two classes of men are always upon earth, & they should be enemies: whoever tries to reconcile them seeks to destroy existence.

Religion is an endeavour to reconcile the two.

Note: Jesus Christ did not wish to unite, but to seperate them, as in the Parable of sheep and goats! & he says: "I came not to send Peace, "but a Sword."

Messiah or Satan or Tempter was formerly thought to be one of the of the Antediluvians who are our Energies.

A Memorable Fancy

AN Angel came to me and said: "O pitiable foolish young man! "O horrible! O dreadful state! consider the hot burning dungeon "thou art preparing for thyself to all eternity, to which thou art "going in such career."

I said: "Perhaps you will be willing to shew me my eternal lot, "& we will contemplate together upon it, and see whether your lot "or mine is most desirable."

58

So he took me thro' a stable & thro' a church & down into the church vault, at the end of which was a mill: thro' the mill we went, and came to a cave: down the winding cavern we groped our tedious way, till a void boundless as a nether sky appear'd beneath us, & we held by the roots of trees and hung over this immensity; but I said: "if you please, we will commit ourselves to this void, and see whether "providence is here also: if you will not, I will:" but he answer'd: "do not presume, O young man, but as we here remain, behold thy "lot which will soon appear when the darkness passes away."

So I remain'd with him, sitting in the twisted root of an oak; he was suspended in a fungus, which hung with the head downward into the deep.

By degrees we beheld the infinite Abyss, fiery as the smoke of a burning city; beneath us, at an immense distance, was the sun, black but shining; round it were fiery tracks on which revolv'd vast spiders, crawling after their prey, which flew, or rather swum, in the infinite deep, in the most terrific shapes of animals sprung from corruption; & the air was full of them, & seem'd composed of them: these are Devils, and are called Powers of the air. I now asked my companion which was my eternal lot? he said: "between the black & white "spiders."

But now, from between the black & white spiders, a cloud and fire burst and rolled thro' the deep, black'ning all beneath, so that the nether deep grew black as a sea, & rolled with a terrible noise; beneath us was nothing now to be seen but a black tempest, till looking east between the clouds & the waves, we saw a cataract of blood mixed with fire, and not many stones' throw from us appear'd and sunk again the scaly fold of a monstrous serpent; at last, to the east, distant about three degrees, appear'd a fiery crest above the waves; slowly it reared like a ridge of golden rocks, till we discover'd two globes of crimson fire, from which the sea fled away in clouds of smoke; and now we saw it was the head of Leviathan; his forehead was divided into streaks of green & purple like those on a tyger's forehead: soon we saw his mouth & red gills hang just above the raging foam, tinging the black deep with beams of blood, advancing toward us with all the fury of a spiritual existence.

My friend the Angel climb'd up from his station into the mill: I remain'd alone; & then this appearance was no more, but I found myself sitting ona pleasant bank beside a river by moonlight, hearing a harper, who sung to the harp; & his theme was: "The man who "never alters his opinion is like standing water, & breeds reptiles "of the mind."

But I arose and sought for the mill, & there I found my Angel, who, surprised, asked me how I escaped?

I answer'd: "All that we saw was owing to your metaphysics; for "when you ran away, I found myself on a bank by moonlight hearing "a harper. But now we have seen my eternal lot, shall I shew you "yours?" he laugh'd at my proposal; but I by force suddenly caught him in my arms, & flew westerly thro' the night, till we were elevated above the earth's shadow; then I flung myself with him directly into the body of the sun; here I clothed myself in white, & taking in my hand Swedenborg's volumes, sunk from the glorious clime, and passed all the planets till we came to saturn: here I stay'd to rest, & then leap'd into the void between saturn & the fixed stars.

"Here," said I, "is your lot, in this space—if space it may be "call'd." Soon we saw the stable and the church, & I took him to the altar and open'd the Bible, and lo! it was a deep pit, into which I descended, driving the Angel before me; soon we saw seven houses of brick; one we enter'd; in it were a number of monkeys, baboons, & all of that species, chain'd by the middle, grinning and snatching at one another, but withheld by the shortness of their chains: however, I saw that they sometimes grew numerous, and then the weak were caught by the strong, and with a grinning aspect, first coupled with, & then devour'd, by plucking off first one limb and then another, till the body was left a helpless trunk; this, after grinning & kissing it with seeming fondness, they devour'd too; and here & there I saw one savourily picking the flesh off his own tail; as the stench terribly annoy'd us both, we went into the mill, & I in my hand brought the skeleton of a body, which in the mill was Aristotle's Analytics.

So the Angel said: "thy phantasy has imposed upon me, & thou "oughtest to be ashamed."

I answer'd: "we impose on one another, & it is but lost time to "converse with you whose works are only Analytics."

¶

OPPOSITION is true Friendship[1].

¶

I HAVE always found that Angels have the vanity to speak of themselves as the only wise; this they do with a confident insolence sprouting from systematic reasoning.

Thus Swedenborg boasts that what he writes is new: tho' it is only the Contents or Index of already publish'd books.

A man carried a monkey about for a shew, & because he was a little wiser than the monkey, grew vain, and conciev'd himself as much

[1] This sentence has been obliterated in some copies of the original.

wiser than seven men. It is so with Swedenborg: he shews the folly of churches, & exposes hypocrites, till he imagines that all are religious, & himself the single one on earth that ever broke a net.

Now hear a plain fact: Swedenborg has not written one new truth. Now hear another: he has written all the old falsehoods.

And now hear the reason. He conversed with Angels who are all religious, & conversed not with Devils who all hate religion, for he was incapable thro' his conceited notions.

Thus Swedenborg's writings are a recapitulation of all superficial opinions, and an analysis of the more sublime—but no further.

Have now another plain fact. Any man of mechanical talents may, from the writings of Paracelsus or Jacob Behmen, produce ten thousand volumes of equal value with Swedenborg's, and from those of Dante or Shakespear an infinite number.

But when he has done this, let him not say that he knows better than his master, for he only holds a candle in sunshine.

A Memorable Fancy

ONCE I saw a Devil in a flame of fire, who arose before an Angel that sat on a cloud, and the Devil utter'd these words:

"The worship of God is: Honouring his gifts in other men, each "according to his genius, and loving the greatest men best: those "who envy or calumniate great men hate God; for there is no other "God."

The Angel hearing this became almost blue; but mastering himself he grew yellow, & at last white, pink, & smiling, and then replied:

"Thou Idolater! is not God One? & is not he visible in Jesus "Christ? and has not Jesus Christ given his sanction to the law of

"ten commandments? and are not all other men fools, sinners, &
"nothings?"

The Devil answer'd: "bray a fool in a morter with wheat, yet shall
"not his folly be beaten out of him; if Jesus Christ is the greatest man,
"you ought to love him in the greatest degree; now hear how he has
"given his sanction to the law of ten commandments: did he not mock
"at the sabbath and so mock the sabbath's God? murder those who
"were murder'd because of him? turn away the law from the woman
"taken in adultery? steal the labor of others to support him? bear
"false witness when he omitted making a defence before Pilate?
"covet when he pray'd for his disciples, and when he bid them shake
"off the dust of their feet against such as refused to lodge them?
"I tell you, no virtue can exist without breaking these ten command-
"ments. Jesus was all virtue, and acted from impulse, not from
"rules."

When he had so spoken, I beheld the Angel, who stretched out his
arms, embracing the flame of fire, & he was consumed and arose as
Elijah.

Note: This Angel, who is now become a Devil, is my particular
friend; we often read the Bible together in its infernal or diabolical
sense, which the world shall have if they behave well.

I have also The Bible of Hell, which the world shall have whether
they will or no.

¶

ONE Law for the Lion & Ox is Oppression.

63

The Everlasting Gospel

Written about 1818

THERE is not one Moral Virtue that Jesus Inculcated but Plato &
Cicero did Inculcate before him; what then did Christ Inculcate?
Forgiveness of Sins. This alone is the Gospel, & this is the Life &
Immortality brought to light by Jesus, Even the Covenant of Jehovah,
which is This: If you forgive one another your Trespasses, so shall
Jehovah forgive you, That he himself may dwell among you; but if
you Avenge, you Murder the Divine Image, & he cannot dwell among
you; because you Murder him he arises again, & you deny that he is
Arisen, & are blind to Spirit.

I

If Moral Virtue was Christianity,
Christ's Pretensions were all Vanity,
And Cai[a]phas & Pilate, Men
Praise Worthy, & the Lion's Den
And not the Sheepfold, Allegories
Of God & Heaven & their Glories.
The Moral Christian is the Cause
Of the Unbeliever & his Laws.
The Roman Virtues, Warlike Fame,
Take Jesus' & Jehovah's Name;
For what is Antichrist but those
Who against Sinners Heaven close
With Iron bars, in Virtuous State,
And Rhadamanthus at the Gate?

What can this Gospel of Jesus be?
What Life & Immortality,
What was it that he brought to Light
That Plato & Cicero did not write?
The Heathen Deities wrote them all,
These Moral Virtues, great & small.
What is the Accusation of Sin
But Moral Virtues' deadly Gin?
The Moral Virtues in their Pride
Did o'er the World triumphant ride
In Wars & Sacrifice for Sin,
And Souls to Hell ran trooping in.
The Accuser, Holy God of All
This Pharisaic Worldly Ball,
Amidst them in his Glory Beams
Upon the Rivers & the Streams.
Then Jesus rose & said to Me,
"Thy Sins are all forgiven thee."
Loud Pilate Howl'd, loud Cai[a]phas yell'd,
When they the Gospel Light beheld.
It was when Jesus said to Me,
"Thy Sins are all forgiven thee."
The Christian trumpets loud proclaim
Thro' all the World in Jesus' name
Mutual forgiveness of each Vice,
And oped the Gates of Paradise.
The Moral Virtues in Great fear
Formed the Cross & Nails & Spear,

And the Accuser standing by
Cried out, "Crucify! Crucify!
"Our Moral Virtues ne'er can be,
"Nor Warlike pomp & Majesty;
"For Moral Virtues all begin
"In the Accusations of Sin,
"And all the Heroic Virtues End
"In destroying the Sinners' Friend.
"Am I not Lucifer the Great,
"And you my daughters in Great State,
"The fruit of my Mysterious Tree
"Of Good & Evil & Misery
"And Death & Hell, which now begin
"On everyone who Forgives Sin?"

[*a*]

THE Vision of Christ that thou dost see
Is my Vision's Greatest Enemy:
Thine has a great hook nose like thine,
Mine has a snub nose like to mine:
Thine is the friend of All Mankind,
Mine speaks in parables to the Blind:
Thine loves the same world that mine hates,
Thy Heaven doors are my Hell Gates.
Socrates taught what Meletus
Loath'd as a Nation's bitterest Curse,
And Caiaphas was in his own Mind
A benefactor to Mankind:
Both read the Bible day & night,
But thou read'st black where I read white.

66

Was Jesus gentle, or did he
Give any marks of Gentility?
When twelve years old he ran away
And left his Parents in dismay.
When after three days' sorrow found,
Loud as Sinai's trumpet sound:
"No Earthly Parents I confess—
"My Heavenly Father's business!
"Ye understand not what I say,
"And, angry, force me to obey."
Obedience is a duty then,
And favour gains with God & Men.
John from the Wilderness loud cried;
Satan gloried in his Pride.
"Come," said Satan, "come away,
"I'll soon see if you'll obey!
"John for disobedience bled,
"But you can turn the stones to bread.
"God's high king & God's high Priest
"Shall Plant their Glories in your breast
"If Caiaphas you will obey,
"If Herod you with bloody Prey
"Feed with the sacrifice, & be
"Obedient, fall down, worship me."
Thunders & lightnings broke around,
And Jesus' voice in thunders' sound:
"Thus I seize the Spiritual Prey.
"Ye smiters with disease, make way.

"I come your King & God to sieze.
"Is God a smiter with disease?"
The God of this World raged in vain:
He bound Old Satan in his Chain,
And bursting forth, his furious ire
Became a Chariot of fire.
Throughout the land he took his course,
And traced diseases to their source:
He curs'd the Scribe & Pharisee,
Trampling down Hipocrisy:
Where'er his Chariot took its way,
There Gates of death let in the day,
Broke down from every Chain & Bar;
And Satan in his Spiritual War
Drag'd at his Chariot wheels: loud howl'd
The God of this World: louder roll'd
The Chariot Wheels, & louder still
His voice was heard from Zion's hill,
And in his hand the Scourge shone bright;
He scourg'd the Merchant Canaanite
From out the Temple of his Mind,
And in his Body tight does bind
Satan & all his Hellish Crew;
And thus with wrath he did subdue
The Serpent Bulk of Nature's dross,
Till He had nail'd it to the Cross.
He took on Sin in the Virgin's Womb,
And put it off on the Cross & Tomb
To be Worship'd by the Church of Rome.

Was Jesus Humble? or did he
Give any proofs of Humility?
When but a Child he ran away
And left his Parents in dismay.
When they had wonder'd three days long
These were the words upon his Tongue:
"No Earthly Parents I confess:
"I am doing my Father's business."
When the rich learned Pharisee
Came to consult him secretly,
Upon his heart with Iron pen
He wrote, "Ye must be born again."
He was too Proud to take a bribe;
He spoke with authority, not like a Scribe.
He says with most consummate Art,
"Follow me, I am meek & lowly of heart,"
As that is the only way to Escape
The Miser's net & the Glutton's trap.
He who loves his Enemies, hates his Friends;
This is surely not what Jesus intends;
He must mean the meer love of Civility,
And so he must mean concerning Humility;
But he acts with triumphant, honest pride,
And this is the Reason Jesus died.
If he had been Antichrist, Creeping Jesus,
He'd have done anything to please us:
Gone sneaking into the Synagogues
And not used the Elders & Priests like Dogs,

But humble as a Lamb or an Ass,
Obey himself to Caiaphas.
God wants not Man to humble himself:
This is the Trick of the Ancient Elf.
Humble toward God, Haughty toward Man,
This is the Race that Jesus ran,
And when he humbled himself to God,
Then descended the cruel rod.
"If thou humblest thyself, thou humblest me;
"Thou also dwelst in Eternity.
"Thou art a Man, God is no more,
"Thine own Humanity learn to Adore
"And thy Revenge Abroad display
"In terrors at the Last Judgment day.
"God's Mercy & Long Suffering
"Are but the Sinner to Judgment to bring.
"Thou on the Cross for them shalt pray
"And take Revenge at the last Day.

"Do what you will, this Life's a Fiction
"And is made up of Contradiction."

[d]

Was Jesus Humble? or did he
Give any Proofs of Humility?
Boast of high Things with Humble tone,
And give with Charity a Stone?
When but a Child he ran away
And left his Parents in dismay.

When they had wander'd three days long
These were the words upon his tongue:
"No Earthly Parents I confess:
"I am doing my Father's business."
When the rich learned Pharisee
Came to consult him secretly,
Upon his heart with Iron pen
He wrote, "Ye must be born again."
He was too proud to take a bribe;
He spoke with authority, not like a Scribe.
He says with most consummate Art,
"Follow me, I am meek & lowly of heart,"
As that is the only way to escape
The Miser's net & the Glutton's trap.
What can be done with such desperate Fools
Who follow after the Heathen Schools?
I was standing by when Jesus died;
What I call'd Humility, they call'd Pride.
He who loves his Enemies betrays his Friends;
This surely is not what Jesus intends,
But the sneaking Pride of Heroic Schools,
And the Scribes' & Pharisees' Virtuous Rules;
For he acts with honest, triumphant Pride,
And this is the cause that Jesus died.
He did not die with Christian Ease,
Asking pardon of his Enemies:
If he had, Caiaphas would forgive;
Sneaking submission can always live.
He had only to say that God was the devil,

And the devil was God, like a Christian Civil:
Mild Christian regrets to the devil confess
For affronting him thrice in the Wilderness;
He had soon been bloody Caesar's Elf,
And at last he would have been Caesar himself.
Like dr. Priestly & Bacon & Newton—
Poor Spiritual Knowledge is not worth a button!
For thus the Gospel Sir Isaac confutes:
"God can only be known by his Attributes;
"And as for the Indwelling of the Holy Ghost
"Or of Christ & his Father, it's all a boast
"And Pride & Vanity of the imagination,
"That disdains to follow this World's Fashion."
To teach doubt & Experiment
Certainly was not what Christ meant.
What was he doing all that time,
From twelve years old to manly prime?
Was he then Idle, or the Less
About his Father's business?
Or was his wisdom held in scorn
Before his wrath began to burn
In Miracles throughout the Land,
That quite unnerv'd Caiaphas' hand?
If he had been Antichrist, Creeping Jesus,
He'd have done any thing to please us—
Gone sneaking into Synagogues
And not us'd the Elders & Priests like dogs,
But Humble as a Lamb or Ass
Obey'd himself to Caiaphas.

God wants not Man to Humble himself:
This is the trick of the ancient Elf.
This is the Race that Jesus ran:
Humble to God, Haughty to Man,
Cursing the Rulers before the People
Even to the temple's highest Steeple;
And when he Humbled himself to God,
Then descended the Cruel Rod.
"If thou humblest thyself, thou humblest me;
"Thou also dwell'st in Eternity.
"Thou art a Man, God is no more,
"Thy own humanity learn to adore,
"For that is my Spirit of Life.
"Awake, arise to Spiritual Strife
"And thy Revenge abroad display
"In terrors at the Last Judgment day
"God's Mercy & Long Suffering
"Is but the Sinner to Judgment to bring.
"Thou on the Cross for them shalt pray
"And take Revenge at the Last Day.
"This Corporeal life's a fiction
"And is made up of Contradiction."
Jesus replied & thunders hurl'd:
"I never will Pray for the World.
"Once I did so when I pray'd in the Garden;
"I wish'd to take with me a Bodily Pardon."
Can that which was of woman born
In the absence of the Morn,
When the Soul fell into Sleep

And Archangels round it weep,
Shooting out against the Light
Fibres of a deadly night,
Reasoning upon its own dark Fiction,
In doubt which is Self Contradiction?
Humility is only doubt,
And does the Sun & Moon blot out,
Rooting over with thorns & stems
The buried Soul & all its Gems.
This Life's dim Windows of the Soul
Distorts the Heavens from Pole to Pole
And leads you to Believe a Lie
When you see with, not thro', the Eye
That was born in a night to perish in a night,
When the Soul slept in the beams of Light.
Was Jesus Chaste? or did he, &c.

[e]

Was Jesus Chaste? or did he
Give any Lessons of Chastity?
The morning blush'd fiery red:
Mary was found in Adulterous bed;
Earth groan'd beneath, & Heaven above
Trembled at discovery of Love.
Jesus was sitting in Moses' Chair,
They brought the trembling Woman There.
Moses commands she be stoned to death,
What was the sound of Jesus' breath?
He laid His hand on Moses' Law:

The Ancient Heavens, in Silent Awe
Writ with Curses from Pole to Pole,
All away began to roll:
The Earth trembling & Naked lay
In secret bed of Mortal Clay,
On Sinai felt the hand divine
Putting back the bloody shrine,
And she heard the breath of God
As she heard by Eden's flood:
"Good & Evil are no more!
"Sinai's trumpets, cease to roar!
"Cease, finger of God, to write!
"The Heavens are not clean in thy Sight.
"Thou art Good, & thou Alone;
"Nor may the sinner cast one stone.
"To be Good only, is to be
"A God or else a Pharisee.
"Thou Angel of the Presence Divine
"That didst create this Body of Mine,
"Wherefore hast thou writ these Laws
"And Created Hell's dark jaws?
"My Presence I will take from thee:
"A Cold Leper thou shalt be.
"Tho' thou wast so pure & bright
"That Heaven was Impure in thy Sight,
"Tho' thy Oath turn'd Heaven Pale,
"Tho' thy Covenant built Hell's Jail,
"Tho' thou didst all to Chaos roll
"With the Serpent for its soul,

76

"Still the breath Divine does move
"And the breath Divine is Love.
"Mary, Fear Not! Let me see
"The Seven Devils that torment thee:
"Hide not from my Sight thy Sin,
"That forgiveness thou maist win.
"Has no Man Condemned thee?"
"No Man, Lord:" "then what is he
"Who shall Accuse thee? Come Ye forth,
"Fallen fiends of Heav'nly birth
"That have forgot your Ancient love
"And driven away my trembling Dove.
"You shall bow before her feet;
"You shall lick the dust for Meat;
"And tho' you cannot Love, but Hate,
"Shall be beggars at Love's Gate.
"What was thy love? Let me see it;
"Was it love or dark deceit?"
"Love too long from Me has fled;
"'Twas dark deceit, to Earn my bread;
"'Twas Covet, or 'twas Custom, or
"Some trifle not worth caring for;
"That they may call a shame & Sin
"Love's temple that God dwelleth in,
"And hide in secret hidden shrine
"The Naked Human form divine,
"And render that a Lawless thing
"On which the Soul Expands its wing.
"But this, O Lord, this was my Sin

78

"When first I let these devils in
"In dark pretence to Chastity:
"Blaspheming Love, blaspheming thee.
"Thence Rose Secret Adulteries,
"And thence did Covet also rise.
"My sin thou hast forgiven me,
"Canst thou forgive my Blasphemy?
"Canst thou return to this dark Hell,
"And in my burning bosom dwell?
"And canst thou die that I may live?
"And canst thou Pity & forgive?"
Then Roll'd the shadowy Man away
From the Limbs of Jesus, to make them his prey,
An Ever devouring appetite
Glittering with festering venoms bright,
Crying, "Crucify this cause of distress,
"Who don't keep the secrets of holiness!
"All Mental Powers by Diseases we bind,
"But he heals the deaf & the dumb & the Blind.
"Whom God has afflicted for Secret Ends,
"He Comforts & Heals & calls them Friends."
But, when Jesus was Crucified,
Then was perfected his glitt'ring pride:
In three Nights he devour'd his prey,
And still he devours the Body of Clay;
For dust & Clay is the Serpent's meat,
Which never was made for Man to Eat.

[f]

I am sure this Jesus will not do
Either for Englishman or Jew.

[g]

Seeing this False Christ, In fury & Passion
I made my Voice heard all over the Nation.
What are those, &c.[1]

[h]

This was spoke by My Spectre to Voltaire, Bacon, &c.

Did Jesus teach doubt? or did he
Give any lessons of Philosophy,
Charge Visionaries with deceiving,
Or call Men wise for not Believing?

[i]

Was Jesus Born of a Virgin Pure
With narrow Soul & looks demure?
If he intended to take on Sin
The Mother should an Harlot been,
Just such a one as Magdalen
With seven devils in her Pen;
Or were Jew Virgins still more Curst,
And more sucking devils nurst?
Or what was it which he took on
That he might bring Salvation?
A Body subject to be Tempted,
From neither pain nor grief Exempted?
Or such a body as might not feel

[1]The rest of this passage is lost.

80

The passions that with Sinners deal?
Yes, but they say he never fell.
Ask Caiaphas; for he can tell.
"He mock'd the Sabbath, & he mock'd
"The Sabbath's God, & he unlock'd
"The Evil spirits from their Shrines,
"And turn'd Fishermen to Divines;
"O'erturn'd the Tent of Secret Sins,
"& its Golden cords & Pins—
" 'Tis the Bloody Shrine of War
"Pinn'd around from Star to Star,
"Halls of justice, hating Vice,
"Where the devil Combs his lice.
"He turn'd the devils into Swine
"That he might tempt the Jews to dine;
"Since which, a Pig has got a look
"That for a Jew may be mistook.
" 'Obey your parents.'—What says he?
" 'Woman, what have I to do with thee?
" 'No Earthly Parents I confess:
" 'I am doing my Father's Business.'
"He scorn'd Earth's Parents, scorn'd Earth's God,
"And mock'd the one & the other's Rod;
"His Seventy Disciples sent
"Against Religion & Government:
"They by the Sword of Justice fell
"And him their Cruel Murderer tell.
"He left his Father's trade to roam
"A wand'ring Vagrant without Home;

81

"And thus he others' labour stole
"That he might live above Controll.
"The Publicans & Harlots he
"Selected for his Company,
"And from the Adulteress turn'd away
"God's righteous Law, that lost its Prey."

There is no natural religion
FIRST SERIES
Etched about 1788

THE *Argument*: Man has no notion of moral fitness but from Education. Naturally he is only a natural organ subject to Sense.

I: Man cannot naturally Perceive but through his natural or bodily organs.

II: Man by his reasoning power can only compare & judge of what he has already perciev'd.

III: From a perception of only 3 senses or 3 elements none could deduce a fourth or fifth.

IV: None could have other than natural or organic thoughts if he had none but organic perceptions.

V: Man's desires are limited by his perceptions, none can desire what he has not perciev'd.

VI: The desires & perceptions of man, untaught by any thing but organs of sense, must be limited to objects of sense.

Conclusion: If it were not for the Poetic or Prophetic character the Philosophic & Experimental would soon be at the ratio of all things, & stand still, unable to do other than repeat the same dull round over again.

There is no natural religion
SECOND SERIES
Etched about 1788

I: Man's perceptions are not bounded by organs of perception; he perceives more than sense (tho' ever so acute) can discover.

II: Reason, or the ratio of all we have already known, is not the same that it shall be when we know more.

III: [*This proposition has been lost.*]

IV: The bounded is loathed by its possessor. The same dull round, even of a universe, would soon become a mill with complicated wheels.

V: If the many become the same as the few when possess'd, More! More! is the cry of a mistaken soul; less than All cannot satisfy Man.

VI: If any could desire what he is incapable of possessing, despair must be his eternal lot.

VII: The desire of Man being Infinite, the possession is Infinite & himself Infinite.

Application: He who sees the Infinite in all things, sees God. He who sees the Ratio only, sees himself only.

Therefore God becomes as we are, that we may be as he is.

All religions are one
Etched about 1788

The Voice of one crying in the Wilderness

THE *Argument*: As the true method of knowledge is experiment, the true faculty of knowing must be the faculty which experiences. This faculty I treat of.

PRINCIPLE 1st: That the Poetic Genius is the true Man, and that the body or outward form of Man is derived from the Poetic Genius. Likewise that the forms of all things are derived from their Genius, which by the Ancients was call'd an Angel & Spirit & Demon.

PRINCIPLE 2d: As all men are alike in outward form, So (and with the same infinite variety) all are alike in the Poetic Genius.

PRINCIPLE 3d: No man can think, write, or speak from his heart, but he must intend truth. Thus all sects of Philosophy are from the Poetic Genius adapted to the weaknesses of every individual.

PRINCIPLE 4th: As none by traveling over known lands can find out the unknown, So from already acquired knowledge Man could not acquire more: therefore an universal Poetic Genius exists.

PRINCIPLE 5th: The Religions of all Nations are derived from each Nation's different reception of the Poetic Genius, which is every where call'd the Spirit of Prophecy.

PRINCIPLE 6th: The Jewish & Christian Testaments are An original derivation from the Poetic Genius; this is necessary from the confined nature of bodily sensation.

PRINCIPLE 7th: As all men are alike (tho' infinitely various), So all Religions &, as all similars, have one source.

The true Man is the source, he being the Poetic Genius.

VISIONS OF THE DAUGHTERS OF ALBION

The Eye sees more than the Heart knows

Etched 1793

The Argument

I LOVED Theotormon,
And I was not ashamed;
I trembled in my virgin fears,
And I hid in Leutha's vale!

I plucked Leutha's flower,
And I rose up from the vale;
But the terrible thunders tore
My virgin mantle in twain

Visions

ENSLAV'D, the Daughters of Albion weep; a trembling lamentation
Upon their mountains; in their valleys, sighs toward America.

For the soft soul of America, Oothoon, wander'd in woe,
Along the vales of Leutha seeking flowers to comfort her;
And thus she spoke to the bright Marygold of Leutha's vale:

"Art thou a flower? art thou a nymph? I see thee now a flower,
"Now a nymph! I dare not pluck thee from thy dewy bed!"

The Golden nymph replied: "Pluck thou my flower, Oothoon the
    mild!
"Another flower shall spring, because the soul of sweet delight

"Can never pass away." She ceas'd, & clos'd her golden shrine.

Then Oothoon pluck'd the flower, saying: "I pluck thee from thy bed,
"Sweet flower, and put thee here to glow between my breasts,
"And thus I turn my face to where my whole soul seeks."

Over the waves she went in wing'd exulting swift delight,
And over Theotormon's reign took her impetuous course.

Bromion rent her with his thunders; on his stormy bed
Lay the faint maid, and soon her woes appall'd his thunders hoarse.

Bromion spoke: "Behold this harlot here on Bromion's bed,
"And let the jealous dolphins sport around the lovely maid!
"Thy soft American plains are mine, and mine thy north & south:
"Stampt with my signet are the swarthy children of the sun;
"They are obedient, they resist not, they obey the scourge;
"Their daughters worship terrors and obey the violent.
"Now thou maist marry Bromion's harlot, and protect the child
"Of Bromion's rage, that Oothoon shall put forth in nine moons'
    time."

Then storms rent Theotormon's limbs: he roll'd his waves around
And folded his black jealous waters round the adulterate pair.
Bound back to back in Bromion's caves, terror & meekness dwell:

At entrance Theotormon sits, wearing the threshold hard
With secret tears; beneath him sound like waves on a desart shore
The voice of slaves beneath the sun, and children bought with money,
That shiver in religious caves beneath the burning fires
Of lust, that belch incessant from the summits of the earth.

Oothoon weeps not; she cannot weep! her tears are locked up;
But she can howl incessant writhing her soft snowy limbs
And calling Theotormon's Eagles to prey upon her flesh.

"I call with holy voice! Kings of the sounding air,
"Rend away this defiled bosom that I may reflect
"The image of Theotormon on my pure transparent breast."

The Eagles at her call descend & rend their bleeding prey:
Theotormon severely smiles; her soul reflects the smile,
As the clear spring, mudded with feet of beasts, grows pure & smiles.

The Daughters of Albion hear her woes, & eccho back her sighs.

"Why does my Theotormon sit weeping upon the threshold,
"And Oothoon hovers by his side, perswading him in vain?
"I cry: arise, O Theotormon! for the village dog
"Barks at the breaking day; the nightingale has done lamenting;
"The lark does rustle in the ripe corn, and the Eagle returns
"From nightly prey and lifts his golden beak to the pure east,
"Shaking the dust from his immortal pinions to awake
"The sun that sleeps too long. Arise, my Theotormon, I am pure
"Because the night is gone that clos'd me in its deadly black.

"They told me that the night & day were all that I could see;
"They told me that I had five senses to inclose me up,
"And they inclos'd my infinite brain into a narrow circle,
"And sunk my heart into the Abyss, a red, round globe, hot burning,
"Till all from life I was obliterated and erased.
"Instead of morn arises a bright shadow, like an eye
"In the eastern cloud; instead of night a sickly charnel house:

"That Theotormon hears me not! to him the night and morn
"Are both alike; a night of sighs, a morning of fresh tears,
"And none but Bromion can hear my lamentations.

"With what sense is it that the chicken shuns the ravenous hawk?
"With what sense does the tame pigeon measure out the expanse?
"With what sense does the bee form cells? have not the mouse & frog
"Eyes and ears and sense of touch? yet are their habitations
"And their pursuits as different as their forms and as their joys.
"Ask the wild ass why he refuses burdens, and the meek camel
"Why he loves man: is it because of eye, ear, mouth, or skin,
"Or breathing nostrils? No, for these the wolf and tyger have.
"Ask the blind worm the secrets of the grave, and why her spires
"Love to curl round the bones of death; and ask the rav'nous snake
"Where she gets poison, & the wing'd eagle why he loves the sun;
"And then tell me the thoughts of man, that have been hid of old.

"Silent I hover all the night, and all day could be silent
"If Theotormon once would turn his loved eyes upon me.
"How can I be defil'd when I reflect thy image pure?
"Sweetest the fruit that the worm feeds on, & the soul prey'd on by
        woe,
"The new wash'd lamb ting'd with the village smoke, & the bright
        swan
"By the red earth of our immortal river. I bathe my wings,
"And I am white and pure to hover round Theotormon's breast."

Then Theotormon broke his silence, and he answered:—
"Tell me what is the night or day to one o'erflow'd with woe?
"Tell me what is a thought, & of what substance is it made?

89

"Tell me what is a joy, & in what gardens do joys grow?
"And in what rivers swim the sorrows? and upon what mountains
"Wave shadows of discontent? and in what houses dwell the
    wretched,
"Drunken with woe forgotten, and shut up from cold despair?

"Tell me where dwell the thoughts forgotten till thou call them
    forth?
"Tell me where dwell the joys of old? & where the ancient loves,
"And when will they renew again, & the night of oblivion past,
"That I might traverse time & spaces far remote, and bring
"Comforts into a present sorrow and a night of pain?
"Where goest thou, O thought? to what remote land is thy flight?
"If thou returnest to the present moment of affliction
"Wilt thou bring comforts on thy wings, and dews and honey and
    balm,
"Or poison from the desart wilds, from the eyes of the envier?"

Then Bromion said, and shook the cavern with his lamentation:

"Thou knowest that the ancient trees seen by thine eyes have fruit,
"But knowest thou that trees and fruits flourish upon the earth
"To gratify senses unknown? trees, beasts and birds unknown;
"Unknown, not unperciev'd, spread in the infinite microscope,
"In places yet unvisited by the voyager, and in worlds
"Over another kind of seas, and in atmospheres unknown:
"Ah! are there other wars beside the wars of sword and fire?
"And are there other sorrows beside the sorrows of poverty?
"And are there other joys beside the joys of riches and ease?
"And is there not one law for both the lion and the ox?

"And is there not eternal fire and eternal chains
"To bind the phantoms of existence from eternal life?"

Then Oothoon waited silent all the day and all the night;
But when the morn arose, her lamentation renew'd.
The Daughters of Albion hear her woes, & eccho back her sighs.

"O Urizen! Creator of men! mistaken Demon of heaven!
"Thy joys are tears, thy labour vain to form men to thine image.
"How can one joy absorb another? are not different joys
"Holy, eternal, infinite? and each joy is a Love.

"Does not the great mouth laugh at a gift, & the narrow eyelids mock
"At the labour that is above payment? and wilt thou take the ape
"For thy councellor, or the dog for a schoolmaster to thy children?
"Does he who contemns poverty and he who turns with abhorrence
"From usury feel the same passion, or are they moved alike?
"How can the giver of gifts experience the delights of the merchant?
"How the industrious citizen the pains of the husbandman?
"How different far the fat fed hireling with hollow drum,
"Who buys whole corn fields into wastes, and sings upon the heath!
"How different their eye and ear! how different the world to them!
"With what sense does the parson claim the labour of the farmer?
"What are his nets & gins & traps; & how does he surround him
"With cold floods of abstraction, and with forests of solitude,
"To build him castles and high spires, where kings & priests may
       dwell;
"Till she who burns with youth, and knows no fixed lot, is bound
"In spells of law to one she loaths? and must she drag the chain
"Of life in weary lust? must chilling, murderous thoughts obscure

91

"The clear heaven of her eternal spring; to bear the wintry rage
"Of a harsh terror, driv'n to madness, bound to hold a rod
"Over her shrinking shoulders all the day, & all the night
"To turn the wheel of false desire, and longings that wake her womb
"To the abhorred birth of cherubs in the human form,
"That live a pestilence & die a meteor, & are no more;
"Till the child dwell with one he hates, and do the deed he loaths,
"And the impure scourge force his seed into its unripe birth
"Ere yet his eyelids can behold the arrows of the day?

"Does the whale worship at thy footsteps as the hungry dog;
"Or does he scent the mountain prey because his nostrils wide
"Draw in the ocean? does his eye discern the flying cloud
"As the raven's eye? or does he measure the expanse like the vulture?
"Does the still spider view the cliffs where eagles hide their young;
"Or does the fly rejoice because the harvest is brought in?
"Does not the eagle scorn the earth & despise the treasures beneath?
"But the mole knoweth what is there, & the worm shall tell it thee.
"Does not the worm erect a pillar in the mouldering church yard
"And a palace of eternity in the jaws of the hungry grave?
"Over his porch these words are written: 'Take thy bliss, O Man!
" 'And sweet shall be thy taste, & sweet thy infant joys renew!'

"Infancy! fearless, lustful, happy, nestling for delight
"In laps of pleasure: Innocence! honest, open, seeking
"The vigorous joys of morning light; open to virgin bliss.
"Who taught thee modesty, subtil modesty, child of night & sleep?
"When thou awakest wilt thou dissemble all thy secret joys,
"Or wert thou not awake when all this mystery was disclos'd?

92

"Then com'st thou forth a modest virgin, knowing to dissemble,
"With nets found under thy night pillow, to catch virgin joy
"And brand it with the name of whore, & sell it in the night,
"In silence, ev'n without a whisper, and in seeming sleep.
"Religious dreams and holy vespers light thy smoky fires:
"Once were thy fires lighted by the eyes of honest morn.
"And does my Theotormon seek this hypocrite modesty,
"This knowing, artful, secret, fearful, cautious, trembling hypocrite?
"Then is Oothoon a whore indeed! and all the virgin joys
"Of life are harlots, and Theotormon is a sick man's dream;
"And Oothoon is the crafty slave of selfish holiness.

"But Oothoon is not so: a virgin fill'd with virgin fancies,
"Open to joy and to delight where ever beauty appears;
"If in the morning sun I find it, there my eyes are fix'd
"In happy copulation; if in evening mild, wearied with work,
"Sit on a bank and draw the pleasures of this free born joy.

"The moment of desire! the moment of desire! The virgin
"That pines for man shall awaken her womb to enormous joys
"In the secret shadows of her chamber: the youth shut up from
"The lustful joy shall forget to generate & create an amorous image
"In the shadows of his curtains and in the folds of his silent pillow.
"Are not these the places of religion, the rewards of continence,
"The self enjoyings of selfdenial? why dost thou seek religion?
"Is it because acts are not lovely that thou seekest solitude
"Where the horrible darkness is impressed with reflections of desire?

"Father of Jealousy, be thou accursed from the earth!
"Why hast thou taught my Theotormon this accursed thing?

93

"Till beauty fades from off my shoulders, darken'd and cast out,
"A solitary shadow wailing on the margin of non-entity.

"I cry: Love! Love! Love! happy happy Love! free as the mountain
    wind!
"Can that be Love that drinks another as a sponge drinks water,
"That clouds with jealousy his nights, with weepings all the day,
"To spin a web of age around him, grey and hoary, dark,
"Till his eyes sicken at the fruit that hangs before his sight?
"Such is self-love that envies all, a creeping skeleton
"With lamplike eyes watching around the frozen marriage bed.

"But silken nets and traps of adamant will Oothoon spread,
"And catch for thee girls of mild silver, or of furious gold.
"I'll lie beside thee on a bank & view their wanton play
"In lovely copulation, bliss on bliss, with Theotormon:
"Red as the rosy morning, lustful as the first born beam,
"Oothoon shall view his dear delight, nor e'er with jealous cloud
"Come in the heaven of generous love, nor selfish blightings bring.
"Does the sun walk in glorious raiment on the secret floor
"Where the cold miser spreads his gold; or does the bright cloud
    drop
"On his stone threshold? does his eye behold the beam that brings
"Expansion to the eye of pity? or will he bind himself
"Beside the ox to thy hard furrow? does not that mild beam blot
"The bat, the owl, the glowing tyger, and the king of night?
"The sea fowl takes the wintry blast for a cov'ring to her limbs,
"And the wild snake the pestilence to adorn him with gems & gold;
"And trees & birds & beasts & men behold their eternal joy.

94

"Arise, you little glancing wings, and sing your infant joy!
"Arise, and drink your bliss, for every thing that lives is holy!"

Thus every morning wails Oothoon; but Theotormon sits
Upon the margin'd ocean conversing with shadows dire.

The Daughters of Albion hear her woes, ; eccho back her sighs.

AMERICA
A Prophecy
Etched 1793

PRELUDIUM

THE shadowy Daughter of Urthona stood before red Orc,
When fourteen suns had faintly journey'd o'er his dark abode:
His food she brought in iron baskets, his drink in cups of iron:
Crown'd with a helmet & dark hair the nameless female stood;
A quiver with its burning stores, a bow like that of night,
When pestilence is shot from heaven: no other arms she need!
Invulnerable tho' naked, save where clouds roll round her loins
Their awful folds in the dark air: silent she stood as night;
For never from her iron tongue could voice or sound arise,
But dumb till that dread day when Orc assay'd his fierce embrace.

"Dark Virgin," said the hairy youth, "thy father stern, abhorr'd,
"Rivets my tenfold chains while still on high my spirit soars;
"Sometimes an eagle screaming in the sky, sometimes a lion
"Stalking upon the mountains, & sometimes a whale, I lash
"The raging fathomless abyss; anon a serpent folding
"Around the pillars of Urthona, and round thy dark limbs
"On the Canadian wilds I fold; feeble my spirit folds,
"For chain'd beneath I rend these caverns: when thou bringest food
"I howl my joy, and my red eyes seek to behold thy face—
"In vain! these clouds roll to & fro, & hide thee from my sight."

Silent as despairing love, and strong as jealousy,
The hairy shoulders rend the links; free are the wrists of fire;

97

Round the terrific loins he siez'd the panting, struggling womb;
It joy'd: she put aside her clouds & smiled her first-born smile,
As when a black cloud shews its lightnings to the silent deep.

Soon as she saw the terrible boy, then burst the Virgin cry:

"I know thee, I have found thee, & I will not let thee go:
"Thou art the image of God who dwells in darkness of Africa,
"And thou art fall'n to give me life in regions of dark death."

EUROPE
A Prophecy
Etched 1794

"FIVE windows light the cavern'd Man: thro' one he breathes the air;
"Thro' one hears music of the spheres; thro' one the eternal vine
"Flourishes, that he may recieve the grapes; thro' one can look
"And see small portions of the eternal world that ever groweth;
"Thro' one himself pass out what time he please; but he will not,
"For stolen joys are sweet & bread eaten in secret pleasant."

So sang a Fairy, mocking, as he sat on a streak'd Tulip,
Thinking none saw him: when he ceas'd I started from the trees
And caught him in my hat, as boys knock down a butterfly.
"How know you this," said I, "small Sir? where did you learn this
        song?"
Seeing himself in my possession, thus he answer'd me:
"My master, I am yours! command me, for I must obey."

"Then tell me, what is the material world, and is it dead?"
He, laughing, answer'd: "I will write a book on leaves of flowers,
"If you will feed me on love-thoughts & give me now and then
"A cup of sparkling poetic fancies; so, when I am tipsie,
"I'll sing to you to this soft lute, and shew you all alive
"The world, where every particle of dust breathes forth its joy."

I took him home in my warm bosom: as we went along
Wild flowers I gather'd, & he shew'd me each eternal flower:
He laugh'd aloud to see them whimper because they were pluck'd.
They hover'd round me like a cloud of incense: when I came
Into my parlour and sat down and took my pen to write,
My Fairy sat upon the table and dictated EUROPE.

EUROPE
Vala, or the Four Zoas

"THE joy of woman is the death of her most best beloved
"Who dies for Love of her
"In torments of fierce jealousy & pangs of adoration.
"The Lovers' night bears on my song
"And the nine spheres rejoice beneath my powerful controll.

"They sing unceasing to the notes of my immortal hand.
"The solemn, silent moon
"Reverberates the living harmony upon my limbs,
"The birds & beasts rejoice & play,
"And every one seeks for his mate to prove his inmost joy.

"Furious & terrible they sport & red the nether deep;
"The deep lifts up his rugged head,
"And lost in infinite humming wings vanishes with a cry.
"The fading cry is ever dying,
"The living voice is ever living in its inmost joy.

"Arise, you little glancing wings & sing your infant joy!
"Arise & drink your bliss!
"For every thing that lives is holy; for the source of life
"Descends to be a weeping babe;
"For the Earthworm renews the moisture of the sandy plain.

"Now my left hand I stretch to earth beneath,
"And strike the terrible string.
"I wake sweet joy in dens of sorrow & I plant a smile
"In forests of affliction,
"And wake the bubbling springs of life in regions of dark death.

"O, I am weary! lay thine hand upon me or I faint,
"I faint beneath these beams of thine,
"For thou hast touch'd my five senses & they answer'd thee.
"Now I am nothing, & I sink
"And on the bed of silence sleep till thou awakest me."

"I am made to sow the thistle for wheat, the nettle for a nourishing
        dainty.
"I have planted a false oath in the earth; it has brought forth a poison
    tree.
"I have chosen the serpent for a councellor, & the dog
"For a schoolmaster to my children.
"I have blotted out from light & living the dove & nightingale,
"And I have caused the earth worm to beg from door to door.

"I have taught the thief a secret path into the house of the just.
"I have taught pale artifice to spread his nets upon the morning.
"My heavens are brass, my earth is iron, my moon a clod of clay,
"My sun a pestilence burning at noon & a vapour of death in night.

"What is the price of Experience? do men buy it for a song?
"Or wisdom for a dance in the street? No, it is bought with the price
"Of all that a man hath, his house, his wife, his children.
"Wisdom is sold in the desolate market where none come to buy,
"And in the wither'd field where the farmer plows for bread in vain.

"It is an easy thing to triumph in the summer's sun
"And in the vintage & to sing on the waggon loaded with corn.
"It is an easy thing to talk of patience to the afflicted,

"To speak of the laws of prudence to the houseless wanderer,
"To listen to the hungry raven's cry in wintry season
"When the red blood is fill'd with wine & with the marrow of lambs.

"It is an easy thing to laugh at wrathful elements,
"To hear the dog howl at the wintry door, the ox in the slaughter
 house moan;
"To see a god on every wind & a blessing on every blast;
"To hear sounds of love in the thunder storm that destroys our
 enemies' house;
"To rejoice in the blight that covers his field, & the sickness that
 cuts off his children,
"While our olive & vine sing & laugh round our door, & our children
 bring fruits & flowers.

"Then the groan & the dolor are quite forgotten, & the slave grinding
 at the mill,
"And the captive in chains, & the poor in the prison, & the soldier
 in the field
"When the shatter'd bone hath laid him groaning among the happier
 dead.

"It is an easy thing to rejoice in the tents of prosperity:
"Thus could I sing & thus rejoice: but it is not so with me."

THEN All in Great Eternity Met in the Council of God
As one Man, Even Jesus, upon Gilead & Hermon,
Upon the Limit of Contraction to create the fallen Man.
The Fallen Man stretch'd like a corse upon the oozy Rock,

Wash'd with the tides, pale, overgrown with weeds
That mov'd with horrible dreams; hovering high over his head
Two winged immortal shapes, one standing at his feet
Toward the East, one standing at his head toward the west,
Their wings join'd in the Zenith over head; but other wings
They had which cloth'd their bodies like a garment of soft down,
Silvery white, shining upon the dark blue sky in silver.
Their wings touch'd the heavens; their fair feet hover'd above
The swelling tides; they bent over the dead corse like an arch,
Pointed at top in highest heavens, of precious stones & pearl.
Such is a Vision of All Beulah hov'ring over the Sleeper.

MILTON

AND did those feet in ancient time
Walk upon England's mountains green?
And was the holy Lamb of God
On England's pleasant pastures seen?

And did the Countenance Divine
Shine forth upon our clouded hills?
And was Jerusalem builded here
Among these dark Satanic Mills?

Bring me my Bow of burning gold:
Bring me my Arrows of desire:
Bring me my Spear: O clouds unfold!
Bring me my Chariot of fire.

I will not cease from Mental Fight,
Nor shall my Sword sleep in my hand
Till we have built Jerusalem
In England's green & pleasant Land.

BUT the Wine-press of Los is eastward of Golgonooza before the Seat
Of Satan: Luvah laid the foundation & Urizen finish'd it in howling
    woe.
How red the sons & daughters of Luvah! here they tread the grapes:
Laughing & shouting, drunk with odours many fall o'erwearied,
Drown'd in the wine is many a youth & maiden: those around
Lay them on skins of Tygers & of the spotted Leopard & the Wild Ass
Till they revive, or bury them in cool grots, making lamentation.

This Wine-press is call'd War on Earth: it is the Printing-Press
Of Los, and here he lays his words in order above the mortal brain,
As cogs are form'd in a wheel to turn the cogs of the adverse wheel.

Timbrels & violins sport round the Wine-presses; the little Seed,
The sportive Root, the Earth-worm, the gold Beetle, the wise Emmet
Dance round the Wine-presses of Luvah: the Centipede is there,
The ground Spider with many eyes, the Mole clothed in velvet,
The ambitious Spider in his sullen web, the lucky golden Spinner,
The Earwig arm'd, the tender Maggot, emblem of immortality,
The Flea, Louse, Bug, the Tape-Worm, all the Armies of Disease,
Visible or invisible to the slothful vegetating Man.
The slow Slug, the Grasshopper that sings & laughs & drinks:
Winter comes, he folds his slender bones without a murmur.
The cruel Scorpion is there, the Gnat, Wasp, Hornet & the Honey
    Bee,
The Toad & venomous Newt, the Serpent cloth'd in gems & gold.
They throw off their gorgeous raiment: they rejoice with loud jubilee
Around the Wine-presses of Luvah, naked & drunk with wine.

There is the Nettle that stings with soft down, and there
The indignant Thistle whose bitterness is bred in his milk,
Who feeds on contempt of his neighbour: there all the idle Weeds
That creep around the obscure places shew their various limbs
Naked in all their beauty dancing round the Wine-presses.

But in the Wine-presses the Human grapes sing not nor dance:
They howl & writhe in shoals of torment, in fierce flames consuming,
In chains of iron & in dungeons circled with ceaseless fires,
In pits & dens & shades of death, in shapes of torment & woe:

The plates & screws & wracks & saws & cords & fires & cisterns,
The cruel joys of Luvah's Daughters, lacerating with knives
And whips their Victims, & the deadly sport of Luvah's Sons.

They dance around the dying & they drink the howl & groan,
They catch the shrieks in cups of gold, they hand them to one another:
These are the sports of love, & these the sweet delights of amorous
    play,
Tears of the grape, the death sweat of the cluster, the last sigh
Of the mild youth who listens to the lureing songs of Luvah.

But Allamanda, call'd on Earth Commerce, is the Cultivated land
Around the City of Golgonooza in the Forests of Entuthon:
Here the Sons of Los labour against Death Eternal, through all
The Twenty-seven Heavens of Beulah in Ulro, Seat of Satan,
Which is the False Tongue beneath Beulah: it is the Sense of Touch.
The Plow goes forth in tempests & lightnings, & the Harrow cruel
In blights of the east, the heavy Roller follows in howlings of woe.

Urizen's sons here labour also, & here are seen the Mills
Of Theotormon on the verge of the Lake of Udan-Adan.
These are the starry voids of night & the depths & caverns of earth.
These Mills are oceans, clouds & waters ungovernable in their fury:
Here are the stars created & the seeds of all things planted,
And here the Sun & Moon recieve their fixed destinations.

But in Eternity the Four Arts, Poetry, Painting, Music
And Architecture, which is Science, are the Four Faces of Man.
Not so in Time & Space: there Three are shut out, and only
Science remains thro' Mercy, & by means of Science the Three
Become apparent in Time & Space in the Three Professions,

[Poetry in Religion: Music, Law: Painting, in Physic & Surgery:
    erased]
That Man may live upon Earth till the time of his awaking.
And from these Three Sciences derives every Occupation of Men,
And Science is divided.

THOU hearest the Nightingale begin the Song of Spring.
The Lark sitting upon his earthy bed, just as the morn
Appears, listens silent; then springing from the waving Cornfield,
    loud
He leads the Choir of Day: trill, trill, trill, trill,
Mounting upon the wings of light into the Great Expanse,
Reecchoing against the lovely blue & shining heavenly Shell,
His little throat labours with inspiration; every feather
On throat & breast & wings vibrates with the effluence Divine.
All Nature listens silent to him, & the awful Sun
Stands still upon the Mountain looking on this little Bird
With eyes of soft humility & wonder, love & awe,
Then loud from their green covert all the Birds begin their Song:
The Thrush, the Linnet & the Goldfinch, Robin & the Wren
Awake the Sun from his sweet reverie upon the Mountain.
The Nightingale again assays his song, & thro' the day
And thro' the night warbles luxuriant, every Bird of Song
Attending his loud harmony with admiration & love.
This is a Vision of the lamentation of Beulah over Ololon.

Thou percievest the Flowers put forth their precious Odours,
And none can tell how from so small a center comes such sweets,
Forgetting that within that Center Eternity expands

108

Its ever during doors that Og & Anak fiercely guard.
First, e'er the morning breaks, joy opens in the flowery bosoms,
Joy even to tears, which the Sun rising dries; first the Wild Thyme
And Meadow-sweet, downy & soft waving among the reeds,
Light springing on the air, lead the sweet Dance: they wake
The Honeysuckle sleeping on the Oak; the flaunting beauty
Revels along upon the wind; the White-thorn, lovely May,
Opens her many lovely eyes listening; the Rose still sleeps,
None dare to wake her; soon she bursts her crimson curtain'd bed
And comes forth in the majesty of beauty; every Flower,
The Pink, the Jessamine, the Wall-flower, the Carnation,
The Jonquil, the mild Lilly, opes her heavens; every Tree
And Flower & Herb soon fill the air with an innumerable Dance,
Yet all in order sweet & lovely. Men are sick with Love,
Such is the Vision of the lamentation of Beulah over Ololon.

THERE is a Moment in each Day that Satan cannot find,
Nor can his Watch Fiends find it; but the Industrious find
This Moment & it multiply, & when it once is found
It renovates every Moment of the Day if rightly placed.
In this Moment Ololon descended to Los & Enitharmon
Unseen beyond the Mundane Shell, Southward in Milton's track.

Just in this Moment, when the morning odours rise abroad
And first from the Wild Thyme, stands a Fountain in a rock
Of crystal flowing into two Streams: one flows thro' Golgonooza
And thro' Beulah to Eden beneath Los's western Wall:
The other flows thro' the Aerial Void & all the Churches,
Meeting again in Golgonooza beyond Satan's Seat.

The Wild Thyme is Los's Messenger to Eden, a mighty Demon,
Terrible, deadly & poisonous his presence in Ulro dark;
Therefore he appears only a small Root creeping in grass
Covering over the Rock of Odours his bright purple mantle
Beside the Fount above the Lark's nest in Golgonooza.
Luvah slept here in death & here is Luvah's empty Tomb.
Ololon sat beside this Fountain on the Rock of Odours.

Just at the place to where the Lark mounts is a Crystal Gate:
It is the enterance of the First Heaven, named Luther; for
The Lark is Los's Messenger thro' the Twenty-seven Churches,
That the Seven Eyes of God, who walk even to Satan's Seat
Thro' all the Twenty-seven Heavens, may not slumber nor sleep.
But the Lark's Nest is at the Gate of Los, at the eastern
Gate of wide Golgonooza, & the Lark is Los's Messenger.

WHEN on the highest lift of his light pinions he arrives
At that bright Gate, another Lark meets him, & back to back
They touch their pinions, tip tip, and each descend
To their respective Earths & there all night consult with Angels
Of Providence & with the eyes of God all night in slumbers
Inspired, & at the dawn of day send out another Lark
Into another Heaven to carry news upon his wings.
Thus are the Messengers dispatch'd till they reach the Earth again
In the East Gate of Golgonooza, & the Twenty-eighth bright
Lark met the Female Ololon descending into my Garden.
Thus it appears to Mortal eyes & those of the Ulro Heavens,
But not thus to Immortals: the Lark is a mighty Angel.

110

For Ololon step'd into the Polypus within the Mundane Shell.
They could not step into Vegetable Worlds without becoming
The enemies of Humanity, except in a Female Form,
And as One Female Ololon and all its mighty Hosts
Appear'd, a Virgin of twelve years: nor time nor space was
To the perception of the Virgin Ololon, but as the
Flash of lightning, but more quick the Virgin in my Garden
Before my Cottage stood, for the Satanic Space is delusion.

For when Los join'd with me he took me in his fi'ry whirlwind:
My Vegetated portion was hurried from Lambeth's shades,
He set me down in Felpham's Vale & prepar'd a beautiful
Cottage for me, that in three years I might write all these Visions
To display Nature's cruel holiness, the deceits of Natural Religion.
Walking in my Cottage Garden, sudden I beheld
The Virgin Ololon & address'd her as a Daughter of Beulah:

"Virgin of Providence, fear not to enter into my Cottage.
"What is thy message to thy friend? What am I now to do?
"Is it again to plunge into deeper affliction? behold me
"Ready to obey, but pity thou my Shadow of Delight:
"Enter my Cottage, comfort her, for she is sick with fatigue."

The Virgin answer'd: "Knowest thou of Milton who descended
"Driven from Eternity? him I seek, terrified at my Act
"In Great Eternity which thou knowest: I come him to seek."

JERUSALEM

BEING not irritated by insult, bearing insulting benevolences,
They percieved that corporeal friends are spiritual enemies:
They saw the Sexual Religion in its embryon Uncircumcision,
And the Divine hand was upon them, bearing them thro' darkness
Back safe to their Humanity, as doves to their windows.
Therefore the Sons of Eden praise Urthona's Spectre in Songs,
Because he kept the Divine Vision in time of trouble.

"WHAT may Man be? who can tell! but what may Woman be
"To have power over Man from Cradle to corruptible Grave?
"There is a Throne in every Man, it is the Throne of God;
"This, Woman has claim'd as her own, & Man is no more!
"Albion is the Tabernacle of Vala & her Temple,
"And not the Tabernacle & Temple of the Most High.
"O Albion, why wilt thou Create a Female Will?
"To hide the most evident God in a hidden covert, even
"In the shadows of a Woman & a secluded Holy Place,
"That we may pry after him as after a stolen treasure,
"Hidden among the Dead & mured up from the paths of life.
"Hand! art thou not Reuben enrooting thyself into Bashan
"Till thou remainest a vaporous Shadow in a Void? O Merlin!
"Unknown among the Dead where never before Existence came,
"Is this the Female Will, O ye lovely Daughters of Albion?"

TURNING from Universal Love, petrific as he went,
His cold against the warmth of Eden rag'd with loud
Thunders of deadly war (the fever of the human soul),

Fires and clouds of rolling smoke! but mild, the Saviour follow'd him,
Displaying the Eternal Vision, the Divine Similitude,
In loves and tears of brothers, sisters, sons, fathers and friends,
Which if Man ceases to behold, he ceases to exist,

Saying, "Albion! Our wars are wars of life, & wounds of love
"With intellectual spears, & long winged arrows of thought.
"Mutual in one another's love and wrath all renewing
"We live as One Man; for contracting our infinite senses
"We behold multitude, or expanding, we behold as one,
"As One Man all the Universal Family, and that One Man
"We call Jesus the Christ; and he in us, and we in him
"Live in perfect harmony in Eden, the land of life,
"Giving, recieving, and forgiving each other's trespasses.
"He is the Good shepherd, he is the Lord and master,
"He is the Shepherd of Albion, he is all in all,
"In Eden, in the garden of God, and in heavenly Jerusalem.
"If we have offended, forgive us; take not vengeance against us."

THIS Gate cannot be found
By Satan's Watch-fiends, tho' they search numbering every grain
Of sand on Earth every night, they never find this Gate.
It is the Gate of Los. Withoutside is the Mill, intricate, dreadful
And fill'd with cruel tortures; but no mortal man can find the Mill
Of Satan in his mortal pilgrimage of seventy years,
For Human beauty knows it not, nor can Mercy find it! But
In the Fourth region of Humanity, Urthona nam'd,
Mortality begins to roll the billows of Eternal Death.

113

"BEHOLD, in the Visions of Elohim Jehovah, behold Joseph & Mary
"And be comforted, O Jerusalem, in the Visions of Jehovah Elohim."

She looked & saw Joseph the Carpenter in Nazareth & Mary
His espoused Wife. And Mary said, "If thou put me away from thee
"Dost thou not murder me?" Joseph spoke in anger & fury, "Should I
"Marry a Harlot & an Adulteress?" Mary answer'd, "Art thou more
      pure
"Than thy Maker who forgiveth Sins & calls again Her that is Lost?
"Tho' She hates, he calls her again in love. I love my dear Joseph,
"But he driveth me away from his presence; yet I hear the voice of
      God
"In the voice of my Husband: tho' he is angry for a moment, he
      will not
"Utterly cast me away; if I were pure, never could I taste the sweets
"Of the Forgiveness of Sins; if I were holy, I never could behold the
      tears
"Of love of him who loves me in the midst of his anger in furnace
      of fire."

"Ah my Mary!" said Joseph, weeping over & embracing her closely
      in
His arms: "Doth he forgive Jerusalem, & not exact Purity from her
      who is
"Polluted? I heard his voice in my sleep & his Angel in my dream,
"Saying, 'Doth Jehovah Forgive a Debt only on condition that it shall
" 'Be Payed? Doth he Forgive Pollution only on conditions of Purity?
" 'That Debt is not Forgiven! That Pollution is not Forgiven!
" 'Such is the Forgiveness of the Gods, the Moral Virtues of the

114

" 'Heathen whose tender Mercies are Cruelty. But Jehovah's Salva-
    tion
" 'Is without Money & without Price, in the Continual Forgiveness
    of Sins,
" 'In the Perpetual Mutual Sacrifice in Great Eternity; for behold,
" 'There is none that liveth & Sinneth not! And this is the Covenant
" 'Of Jehovah: If you Forgive one-another, so shall Jehovah Forgive
    You,
" 'That He Himself may Dwell among You. Fear not then to take
" 'To thee Mary thy Wife, for she is with Child by the Holy Ghost.' "

Then Mary burst forth into a Song: she flowed like a River of
Many Streams in the arms of Joseph & gave forth her tears of joy
Like many waters, and Emanating into gardens & palaces upon
Euphrates, & to forests & floods & animals wild & tame from
Gihon to Hiddekel, & to corn fields & villages & inhabitants
Upon Pison & Arnon & Jordan. And I heard the voice among
The Reapers, Saying, "Am I Jerusalem the lost Adulteress? or am I
"Babylon come up to Jerusalem?" And another voice answer'd,
    Saying,

"Does the voice of my Lord call me again? am I pure thro' his Mercy
"And Pity? Am I become lovely as a Virgin in his sight, who am
"Indeed a Harlot drunken with the Sacrifice of Idols? does he
"Call her pure as he did in the days of her Infancy when She
"Was cast out to the loathing of her person? The Chaldean took
"Me from my Cradle. The Amalekite stole me away upon his Camels
"Before I had ever beheld with love the Face of Jehovah, or known
"That there was a God of Mercy. O Mercy, O Divine Humanity!

"O Forgiveness & Pity & Compassion! If I were Pure I should never
"Have known Thee: If I were Unpolluted I should never have
"Glorified thy Holiness or rejoiced in thy great Salvation."

Mary leaned her side against Jerusalem: Jerusalem received
The Infant into her hands in the Visions of Jehovah. Times passed on.

ALBION cold lays on his Rock: storms & snows beat round him,
Beneath the Furnaces & the starry Wheels & the Immortal Tomb:
Howling winds cover him: roaring seas dash furious against him:
In the deep darkness broad lightnings glare, long thunders roll.

The weeds of Death inwrap his hands & feet, blown incessant
And wash'd incessant by the for-ever restless sea-waves foaming
    abroad
Upon the white Rock. England, a Female Shadow, as deadly damps
Of the Mines of Cornwall & Derbyshire, lays upon his bosom heavy,
Moved by the wind in volumes of thick cloud, returning, folding
    round
His loins & bosom, unremovable by swelling storms & loud rending
Of enraged thunders. Around them the Starry Wheels of their Giant
    Sons
Revolve, & over them the Furnaces of Los, & the Immortal Tomb
    around,
Erin sitting in the Tomb to watch them unceasing night and day:
And the Body of Albion was closed apart from all Nations.

   Over them the famish'd Eagle screams on boney Wings, and around
Them howls the Wolf of famine; deep heaves the Ocean black,
    thundering

Around the wormy Garments of Albion, then pausing in deathlike
    silence.

HER voice pierc'd Albion's clay cold ear; he moved upon the Rock.
The Breath Divine went forth upon the morning hills. Albion mov'd
Upon the Rock, he open'd his eyelids in pain, in pain he mov'd
His stony members, he saw England. Ah! shall the Dead live again?

The Breath Divine went forth over the morning hills. Albion rose
In anger, the wrath of God breaking, bright flaming on all sides
    around
His awful limbs; into the Heavens he walked, clothed in flames,
Loud thund'ring, with broad flashes of flaming lightning & pillars
Of fire, speaking the Words of Eternity in Human Forms, in direful
Revolutions of Action & Passion, thro' the Four Elements on all sides
Surrounding his awful Members. Thou seest the Sun in heavy clouds
Struggling to rise above the Mountains; in his burning hand
He takes his Bow, then chooses out his arrows of flaming gold;
Murmuring the Bowstring breathes with ardor! clouds roll round the
Horns of the wide Bow, loud sounding winds sport on the mountain
    brows,
Compelling Urizen to his Furrow & Tharmas to his Sheepfold
And Luvah to his Loom. Urthona he beheld, mighty labouring at
His Anvil, in the Great Spectre Los unwearied labouring & weeping:
Therefore the Sons of Eden praise Urthona's Spectre in songs,
Because he kept the Divine Vision in time of trouble.

As the Sun & Moon lead forward the Visions of Heaven & Earth,
England, who is Brittannia, enter'd Albion's bosom rejoicing,

Rejoicing in his indignation, adoring his wrathful rebuke.
She who adores not your frowns will only loathe your smiles.

AS the Sun & Moon lead forward the Visions of Heaven & Earth,
England, who is Brittannia, entered Albion's bosom rejoicing.

Then Jesus appeared standing by Albion as the Good Shepherd
By the lost Sheep that he hath found, & Albion knew that it
Was the Lord, the Universal Humanity; & Albion saw his Form
A Man, & they conversed as Man with Man in Ages of Eternity.
And the Divine Appearance was the likeness & similitude of Los.

Albion said: "O Lord, what can I do? my Selfhood cruel
"Marches against thee, deceitful, from Sinai & from Edom
"Into the Wilderness of Judah, to meet thee in his pride.
"I behold the Visions of my deadly Sleep of Six Thousand Years
"Dazzling around thy skirts like a Serpent of precious stones & gold.
"I know it is my Self, O my Divine Creator & Redeemer."

Jesus replied: "Fear not Albion: unless I die thou canst not live;
"But if I die I shall arise again & thou with me.
"This is Friendship & Brotherhood: without it Man Is Not."

So Jesus spoke: the Covering Cherub coming on in darkness
Overshadow'd them, & Jesus said: "Thus do Men in Eternity
"One for another to put off, by forgiveness, every sin."

Albion reply'd: "Cannot Man exist without Mysterious
"Offering of Self for Another? is this Friendship & Brotherhood?
"I see thee in the likeness & similitude of Los my Friend."

Jesus said: "Wouldest thou love one who never died
"For thee, or ever die for one who had not died for thee?
"And if God dieth not for Man & giveth not himself
"Eternally for Man, Man could not exist; for Man is Love
"As God is Love: every kindness to another is a little Death
"In the Divine Image, nor can Man exist but by Brotherhood."

So saying the Cloud overshadowing divided them asunder.
Albion stood in terror, not for himself but for his Friend
Divine; & Self was lost in the contemplation of faith
And wonder at the Divine Mercy & at Los's sublime honour.

"Do I sleep amidst danger to Friends? O my Cities & Counties,
"Do you sleep? rouze up, rouze up! Eternal Death is abroad!"

So Albion spoke & threw himself into the Furnaces of affliction.
All was a Vision, all a Dream: the Furnaces became
Fountains of Living Waters flowing from the Humanity Divine.
And all the Cities of Albion rose from their Slumbers, and All
The Sons & Daughters of Albion on soft clouds, waking from Sleep.
Soon all around remote the Heavens burnt with flaming fires,
And Urizen & Luvah & Tharmas & Urthona arose into
Albion's Bosom. Then Albion stood before Jesus in the Clouds
Od Heaven, Fourfold among the Visions of God in Eternity.

THE END

120